NOBODY WANTS TO TALK ABOUT IT

AN ENLIGHTENING GUIDE TO PLANNING A FUNERAL OR OTHER TRIBUTE

George W. Clarke
With
Dennis M. Lo

A BUSINESS & EDUCATIONAL IMPRINT FROM ADDUCENT
www.AdducentInc.com

<u>Titles Distributed In</u>

North America
United Kingdom
Western Europe
South America
Australia

NOBODY WANTS TO TALK ABOUT IT

An Enlightening Guide to Planning a Funeral or Other Tribute

George W. Clarke with Dennis M. Lowery

ISBN: 9781937592400

Published by Booknology (a business and educational imprint from Adducent)

Jacksonville, Florida

www.AdducentInc.com

Published in the United States of America

“Everyone knows they’re going to die,' he said again, 'but nobody believes it.”

-Mitch Albom, *Tuesdays with Morrie*

TABLE OF CONTENTS

DEDICATION

For Gloria and Vern

Acknowledgments

This book is the result of the many years spent working in the funeral profession.

Throughout my career, I have had the privilege to assist many families faced with unspeakable personal tragedy and loss. Their grace, strength, and enduring love for the person they had lost inspired me then and continue to do so today.

Over those years I have also known many funeral directors who are unwavering, compassionate, and dedicated professionals. Their commitment to caring for those who call upon them, and the substantial sacrifices their work exacts on them and their own families, are seldom acknowledged but ever present.

"I've had the privilege and pleasure to work with George Clarke for more than a decade. His abilities bring compassion and insight to the sensitive topics of death, ceremony and life afterward are truly distinct and remarkable, from a career in the funeral services industry working with funeral homes, political groups, federal and state regulatory agencies, media, consumer rights advocates and most importantly, families themselves. George's combination of service and experience and his natural characteristic to communicate clearly and meaningfully uniquely distinguish him as the lone salient information point in a confusing marketplace. He is a must see and must hear speaker on this critically important topic that all too often rears suddenly in our lives without warning or preparation, leaving us to make decisions at the time we are least capable of understanding options, let alone the importance of how to appropriately deal with the event of a death."

Michael P.A. Cohen, Attorney
Chair, Antitrust and
International Competition Practice
Paul Hastings LLP, Washington, DC

"I first met George Clarke when he was the Executive Director for Selected Independent Funeral Homes. George's expertise in the funeral industry is unprecedented! He knows his business and can be trusted. He is a man of integrity, honesty, and loyalty. George is a dynamic public speaker who knows how to engage his audience. He is a wise man with good counsel. George is one of the most consistent, professional people I know. He truly knows how to get things done and would be an asset to any company or business event. George is a team player. I'm proud to call him a friend and a business associate."

Larry Cappetto, Independent Filmmaker
VeteransHistory.org

"With his vast knowledge and understanding of funeral service, George W. Clarke would be an outstanding speaker to consumers about the value of funeral service. As a member of Selected Independent Funeral Homes, I was always impressed with George's understanding of funeral service and in his ability to speak about the values of funeral service. As President of SIFH, I witnessed firsthand how well-spoken George was about all aspects of funeral service. In all venues, whether it was in front of our membership or dealing with the FTC in public hearings or on panel discussions with other leaders of the various trade organizations, George was the most informed and well-spoken individual participating. He has the ability to quickly recognize all sides of an issue and the consequences related in trying to solve that issue. Foremost, George always insisted upon taking the high road and placing ethics above all else in the practice of funeral service."

John Michelotti, President,
Michelotti-Sawyers Mortuary and Crematory
Billings, MT

"In the nearly two decades I have had opportunity to observe George Clarke's work, I have found him to be an extraordinary source of all things relating to funerals! He communicates with integrity and candor—so I never think I needed to double-check my sources. Ironically, he brings an uncanny perspective of both outsider and insider to this unique profession. He knows the business, he understands the intricacies of this unusual profession, and he is a practitioner of the undertaker's art. In my estimation, that gives him a unique perspective on this work."

William G. "Bill" Hoy, Ph.D.
Lecturer, Medical Humanities Program
College of Arts & Sciences, Baylor University
Executive Director, GriefConnect,
www.GriefConnect.com

INTRODUCTION

For more than 30 years, I've been involved in various segments of the funeral industry, from the early days in my role as a funeral director to my more recent 11-year tenure as the executive director of the world's oldest and largest international association of independently owned funeral homes.

I have witnessed the confusion and discomfort that can exist for those responsible for arranging final tributes and services. Throughout my career, one basic concept has remained very clear: informed purchasers of funeral services, as with any product or service, are far more likely to make decisions most appropriate for their unique personal needs and circumstances. Unfortunately, the subjects of death and funerals are so discomforting for many people that they don't collect the information before the need arises. In addition, these decisions have become more confusing for many people due to contemporary factors, such as the distances that separate family members, the virtually unlimited options for personalization of funeral services, and the growing popularity of "green burial" alternatives, to name only a few.

This guide is a source of objective and factual information. In it, I'll share information and insight about the many questions, decisions, and options facing those responsible for arranging tributes and funeral services for those they love. It's neither my wish nor intent to influence personal decisions about any form of final tribute. It's my goal to equip people with information that reduces the potential for miscommunication and regret, and lessens stress during what many describe as the most difficult time in their lives. Near the end of the book, I have provided a summary of the emergency steps to take immediately after a death occurs.

This guide is not intended to be an exposé of the funeral industry. In my years of experience working with funeral home owners and managers throughout North America and in other countries, I have come to respect the vast majority of them as dedicated, committed professionals whose primary objective is to care for those who look to them for assistance. As is the case with all occupations, there are some funeral directors who are seemingly motivated by the desire to take advantage of people when they are perhaps most vulnerable. There are others who may be unqualified, professionally and/or personally, to function legally, ethically, and honorably in their profession. Thankfully, they represent only the tiniest portion of funeral service practitioners, and I hope that this guide will help you to recognize them, avoid doing business with them, and learn how to report serious and unresolvable breaches of conduct to the appropriate authorities.

I do not attempt to examine the psychological aspects of grief and loss. Those topics are best left to those with the credentials and experience to adequately address them.

It's my hope that you'll find this guide helpful as you arrange tributes for yourself or those you care about.

CHAPTER ONE

WE DON'T LIKE TO TALK ABOUT IT (BUT WE SHOULD)

You see them everywhere: advertisements for almost any product or service one could imagine. And many of them are of such a personal nature that not long ago it would have been outrageous to bring them up. But the subjects of death and funerals remain almost unthinkable for many of us, except perhaps in the desensitized, artificial world of crime novels, TV shows and Hollywood productions.

We understand death is unavoidable, but we're not willing or ready to plan, talk about, or consider it. If we did, would it make a difference? How do we begin to face our own mortality? How do we begin the conversations with our families or others who will be most directly affected by the death? What are the things we should know and the questions we should ask? The answers will help us take steps to prepare for that eventual day by planning a tribute that meets family members' emotional, spiritual, cultural, and economic needs. Later in this guide, I will offer a compelling illustration of the ways in which planning a tribute in advance can result in a meaningful and fulfilling experience.

I have worked with family members whose loved ones died under a wide variety of circumstances: sudden death from natural causes, prolonged illness, disease, homicide, suicide, automobile or airplane crashes, fire, etc. Whether those loved ones were parents, spouses, children, or siblings, no one person's loss is more tragic or devastating than anyone else's, in my view, because each of us is affected in different ways. But there is a broad spectrum of emotions tied to the circumstances surrounding a death, including anger, denial, and shock, and the ways in which those emotions are displayed.

One morning, I was called to a hospital room, to talk with young parents whose baby had just died in utero. The mother had suffered a miscarriage when the baby was almost full term. During our conversation, I learned that the parents did not own a cemetery lot, so it would be necessary for them to choose a cemetery. I spent the better part of the day driving from cemetery to cemetery with the father of the baby, looking at different burial lots that were available to them. I don't think that one cemetery was much different than any other, but we spent several hours doing this, and as I look back on it, I think it was his way of trying to cope with the devastating loss and take some action for his son. He just didn't know what else to do.

Some months later, I handled the arrangements for an elderly couple, husband and wife, who were terminally ill. They apparently decided they didn't want to be a burden to their children or face the daunting medical procedures that would be required in any attempt to prolong their lives. So one day, they bought a bottle of wine, wrote a note to their family, sat in their car in their garage, opened the wine, and started the engine. They had arranged to pipe the exhaust into the car with the windows closed. Both died from carbon monoxide poisoning. Obviously, the family had no reason to suspect this was going to occur. They certainly didn't have time to plan for it. Although they were shocked and saddened by what had occurred, I believe they also experienced some level of relief in the knowledge that their parents' future suffering had been avoided, and that they had died on their own terms.

My point in sharing these stories is that death can strike any of us at any time. We are all subject to a telephone call announcing the death of a child, or a sibling, or a parent, without warning. Any of us can be faced with making these decisions, either following someone's prolonged period of illness and suffering, or without a moment's notice. When someone we love dies, we can be overwhelmed with emotions, fears, confusion, and anxiety on levels we may never have imagined. We may feel powerless and vulnerable, yet we're called upon to answer questions and make decisions for which we are unprepared. With modest effort, however, we can help ourselves to be better able to confront some of the aspects of losing someone we love, regardless of the circumstances surrounding the death. While I'm not suggesting it's possible to prepare in every way for these events, you can equip yourself with the basic information that will help you to begin the many steps involved in grieving and toward healing.

One theme you'll hear repeated throughout this guide is that "funerals are for the living." Beyond the theological aspects of various rituals in mainstream religions, I think it should be obvious that funerals are of no benefit to the person who has died. They are rituals for the living, designed to ease the transition from life with the person we love to life without her.

I believe that family discussions are a critical part of funeral planning, and while the thought of having these conversations may not be easy or comfortable, I'm convinced they can be extraordinarily helpful to anyone. They can begin with a simple question, such as, "Have you ever thought about your own funeral?" Or, "I overheard someone talking about planning her own funeral, and I hadn't thought about it before. Have you ever thought about what you'd want yours to be like?" With these few words, I think it's possible to start a conversation that will help clarify the thoughts and preferences of family members. The conversation doesn't have to be depressing or morbid. It probably will be much less emotionally charged than it would be after a death has occurred. The input from everyone involved, all of the family members impacted by the death, can provide the basis for designing a tribute that will reflect, with honor and dignity, the essence of the unique life that has been lived, and it will help the survivors begin the process of bereavement and recovery.

Chapter Two

The Basics of Planning a Tribute

Throughout this book, I frequently use the terms "funeral" and "memorial." In the interest of simplicity, and for our purposes here, the words are interchangeable, depending on your personal preferences.

Technically, however, there is one significant difference between a funeral and memorial service. It may be evident to you, but I think it's important to make the distinction here. Typically, a funeral is a ceremony with the body present, and the casket may be either open or closed. The term memorial service carries with it the connotation that the casket and body are not present, although if the deceased was cremated, the urn containing the "ashes" may be displayed.

A memorial service can provide the family with a greater array of options when choosing the location of the ceremony. It can be held in the funeral home, at a church or other place of worship, or any public place that could accommodate the number of people the family anticipates would attend the ceremony. Later in this guide, we'll talk about the many options people have when designing a ceremony, whether funeral or memorial, that is most appropriate for them.

Planning Ahead

We all plan ahead for many things in life, from education to retirement to health care to insurance. But very few of us ever take the time to consider and plan for what will eventually affect us all; our death. Particularly in our younger years, we like to think we're invincible. To plan or contemplate one's own funeral requires the acknowledgment of our own mortality, which isn't an easy thing for everyone to do. Even those that work in the funeral or healthcare industry and see death virtually every day may subconsciously feel it's something that happens to somebody else. Conceptually, it shouldn't be any more difficult for us to consider our own funeral arrangements than it is for us to purchase a life insurance policy, which requires us to acknowledge the fact we will die someday and our survivors will need to be cared for financially.

Planning in advance, which can be called pre-planning, pre-arrangements, or "preneed" can take several forms. You have probably heard someone make the comment, "I don't care what happens to me after I die. Just burn me or just dig a hole in the backyard and throw me in there. I don't want anybody to go to any trouble." Someone may think that saying, "I told the funeral home owner the last time I was there that he's going to do my funeral when I die," is preplanning. Others take a more active approach, such as "My wife and I talked about exactly what each of us wanted, and while we didn't write anything down, we both agree on the kind of ceremonies we would prefer."

Some people put instructions in writing. A couple will jointly determine what is to be done when one or both of them dies, and prepare written instructions that specifically direct the responsible next of kin regarding their funeral arrangements. It's important that the person responsible is provided with a copy of those instructions, or at least knows where they can be found when the death occurs. Others may incorporate their wishes in a will, but in most jurisdictions, a will may not be legally binding until it has been successfully probated. That process can take some time, especially if the estate is to be contested, so advance directives in a will don't necessarily accomplish what many people think.

There are others who make detailed pre-arrangements with a funeral home. They make an appointment, meet with the funeral director, put specific instructions in writing, and take whatever steps necessary to ensure that all of their wishes are to be followed. Some people will also elect to pay for everything in advance, wanting to relieve family members of any financial responsibilities for the funeral arrangements. More detailed information about this option can be found in the section on prepayment.

Although any of these approaches may be the result of the best intentions, they all leave out one very important factor: the concept that funerals are for the living. As an illustration, consider a scenario where a man comes to the funeral home and says, "I'm here to make arrangements for my own funeral. I don't want anyone to know I've been here. Please don't send anything to my house. My family will only be upset if they know I've done this."

Now fast forward, to the time when this man dies. The family comes to the funeral home with their own ideas about the type of arrangements they feel are most appropriate for their circumstances, only to be told by the funeral director, "Your father or husband was here a couple of years ago and made all of these arrangements for himself." That creates a potential conflict. If the family's wishes are similar to the instructions left by the person himself, then the process is perhaps made easier, but if there is any substantial difference between the prearranged instructions and the family's preferences, complications can result. Family members may now be faced with the difficult decision of choosing arrangements that they see as most appropriate for themselves and their circumstances, or honoring the wishes of the person who has died. It's a scenario that can add significantly to the stress and confusion they are feeling.

To further complicate the situation, in some jurisdictions the wishes of the deceased, if they are in writing, will override the rights of the next of kin. In that case, the funeral home is legally bound to follow the instructions that the person made in advance. In other states, however, the rights of the next of kin (typically in the order of rights of survivorship: spouse, children, parents, siblings, etc.) will supersede whatever advance arrangements the person who has died had specified.

I have seen a number of situations when conflict in the family, whether or not the deceased had made specific pre-arrangements, is quite considerable. On more than one occasion, I've had to intervene during a particularly emotional and contentious meeting with a family by saying to them, "We need to come to some consensus. Perhaps the best thing is for me to excuse myself and let you continue your discussions in private, or suggest that you go home and talk about it, and then come back when you've made some decisions." Until everyone is in agreement, nothing can proceed, especially in the case of cremation since the process is irreversible.

Family communication is vital to the successful completion of this pre-planning process. It's important for people to get together to talk about their preferences and opinions. If you are discussing what arrangements are to be made following your own death, tell your family what you would like, but also give them the opportunity to share their thoughts on what ceremonies might be most helpful for them. Remember that while you may be the "guest of honor," the funeral is not for you. The funeral is designed, in whatever form it takes, to meet the emotional, spiritual, and other needs of the survivors and help them to begin the healing process.

Planning ahead allows people to prepare for the unexpected event, particularly an acute and fatal illness or accident or some other sudden manner of death, and enables them to consider the most appropriate options for them, without the fog of grief and confusion that complicates decision-making. There are many options that present themselves when people are making arrangements for a funeral, from the location and type of ceremony to the type of disposition, and all of those choices require time to consider.

Preplanning also gives people the opportunity to research funeral costs, to choose a funeral home, and to compare services. Ultimately, you should purchase only those items you need and/or want, rather than feeling like you're being forced into buying something you don't want or clearly understand.

People don't make funeral arrangements very often. Statistically, it's once every 12 years or so. So it's quite normal for you to experience feelings of discomfort and vulnerability. By doing some research in advance, you have more time to understand what is required, what your options are, and reduce the feelings of uncertainty and confusion. Simply put, planning ahead can help to restore some sense of control over what can be a truly overwhelming experience.

Selecting a Funeral Home

Prior to the advent of funeral homes, most services were held at homes or churches. I imagine that many readers are at least somewhat familiar with the term "Irish Wake," a period of time during which the deceased would be "laid out" at home, with family members and friends in attendance to say their goodbyes.

Before funeral homes, embalming in the deceased's home was quite common. When the person died, the funeral director would be notified and he and perhaps an assistant would go to the residence and perform the embalming. The casket would be brought to the home and the deceased placed in it. There would then be a period of visitation before the formal funeral service, which would usually take place in a church.

My mother's father had owned a funeral home in Massachusetts, although I never knew him because he died before I was born. Two of my mother's brothers were funeral directors and embalmers, and I can remember, at about five years of age, seeing in my uncle's basement this enormous black bag I knew to be his "embalmer's bag," containing equipment he had used to embalm people who died at home. I was terrified of that bag. And to this day, I am grateful that I was never called upon to embalm anyone in his or her residence.

It's still possible for people to have funerals at home. That's an option available in almost every state in the U.S., and may be seen by some as a practical, meaningful way to provide a last act of love and kindness to someone they care about. There are resources available via the Internet that provide more detail about the various considerations of home funerals. Most people, however, will find it necessary or easier to engage the services of a funeral home.

Selecting the right funeral home is important, because it's increasingly possible to arrange for traditional or non-traditional types of funeral or memorial services that fall well outside what you may regard as the more religion-oriented liturgies and rites that have been prevalent in the past. I recommend choosing a funeral home that demonstrates the professionalism, creativity, sensitivity, and willingness to work with you to design the type of tribute that meets your family's needs and preferences. If in early discussions with a funeral director you hear, "Well, we just don't do things that way here," then depending upon the extent to which your family would like to incorporate that particular facet or approach, it might be a good idea to seek another funeral home more willing to accommodate your specific wishes.

In years past, the decision about which funeral home to call when a family member died was probably not a decision at all. For generations, one funeral home in the community had provided funerals for most, if not all members of a given family, and the loyalty that developed was strong and enduring.

While that is still true for many people, the mobility of today's society has left many without a designated "family" funeral home. People may find themselves in a new community, suddenly faced with the unexpected death of a spouse, child, or other family member, and are completely unfamiliar with the reputations and qualities of the funeral homes in the area. In smaller communities, there may be only one funeral home and the family has little choice. But generally speaking, there are at least two or three options in most communities.

There was significant trend toward consolidation in the funeral industry that began in the 1980s and continued quite actively for nearly twenty years. The "consolidators" started out as privately held, regional companies that would purchase funeral homes from owners who wanted to retire and/or didn't have children who were interested in carrying on the family business. As time went on, these companies became quite large, publicly traded companies that rapidly expanded their holdings throughout the U.S., Canada, and abroad.

When these companies acquired a funeral home, there was usually little outward sign that the ownership had changed. Historically, funeral homes have built their businesses by word of mouth, and most owners view the funeral home's reputation in the community as the firm's greatest asset. As a result, the large companies were interested in maintaining that reputation and hometown feel, and it was not uncommon for the former owner to remain visible in a manager or consultant role.

The overwhelming majority of funeral homes in the U.S. and Canada remain independently owned. Consolidation in the funeral industry continues today, although at a rate that is significantly slower than at its peak. At the time of this writing, the largest publicly traded funeral home company in the U.S., Service Corporation International (SCI), based in Houston, Texas is in the process of paying $1.13 billion to acquire Stewart Enterprises (the industry's second-largest company), headquartered in Metairie, Louisiana. When the deal is complete, SCI will have approximately 1,653 funeral homes and 515 cemeteries in 48 U.S. states, eight Canadian provinces and Puerto Rico.

In the midst of the current "big-box" retail environment, people may presume that the large, publicly traded funeral home companies offer better service at lower prices. But that may not be true, and I suggest that when choosing a funeral home, people should take the time they need to compare for service, price, and value. I have heard it said many times that the first obligation of the consolidators, as publicly traded companies, is to Wall Street and their shareholders, while the priority of independently owned funeral homes is to Main Street and their communities.

In some states, funeral homes that are owned by the consolidators are required to disclose that fact in their advertising, but in most areas, the identity of the owner may not be as it appears. If it's important to you to deal with an independently or family owned funeral home, I suggest you simply inquire about the funeral home's ownership early in your conversations with the funeral director. You may be surprised by the answer.

If you are among those who have experience with and/or a preference for a particular funeral home, your decision may have already been made, although reading the rest of this section may be helpful. If you haven't determined which funeral home you would call in an emergency, consider the following steps:

Don't wait. Start the process today, while you have time and before the need arises. Ask friends, coworkers, clergy, and other community professionals about their experiences, good and bad.

Telephone several funeral homes in your area. Begin by telling the person you are speaking with that you are in the process of selecting a funeral home, and ask general questions about the funeral home's history in the community and why that funeral home would be the right choice for you. The purpose of this conversation is to get a sense of the staff's attitude, knowledge, courtesy, and professionalism. It doesn't take very long to develop an initial feeling about whether the funeral home may be an option for you. You may also ask about the charges for various services the funeral home can provide. As I'll explain later in this guide, the U.S. Federal Trade Commission requires funeral homes to provide price information over the telephone when the caller requests it.

After completing your initial telephone research, schedule an appointment with one or more of the funeral homes that you feel might be best for you. During that meeting, you should take the opportunity to tour the facility, learn more about the options available to you, and get specific price information for the arrangements you are considering.

Funeral homes usually view this meeting as a pre-arrangement conference, and it is not necessary to pay them any money at the time of your appointment with them. Building their preneed business in important to most funeral homes because it's seen as a method of ensuring their ongoing success. When the death occurs, or at the time of prepayment (if you choose to do so), the funeral home will apply its usual charges for providing the services, which will include an amount for the arrangements conference.

In some circumstances, particularly in rural or suburban areas, it may occur that when someone dies, as a result of an accident, for example, the medical examiner or coroner may order that the body be transported to a designated funeral home until the cause and manner of death are determined. It may be that the funeral home to which the body was transported is not the funeral home the family would have chosen. In that event, when the body has been released by the medical examiner, you are entitled to call the funeral home you prefer and ask them to make arrangements for the body to be transferred.

Similarly, if there are conflicts with a funeral home you have chosen and no resolution can be reached, you should feel empowered to choose another funeral home. All you need to do is make it clear to the funeral director that you will be making other arrangements. You should simply leave the funeral home, contact the other one you have chosen, and ask them to make arrangements for the remains to be transferred to their facility. There may be some charges involved, particularly if the initial funeral home made the transfer from the place of death to the funeral home, or if embalming was performed at the direction of the family. It's not unreasonable for the funeral home to be paid for the services they provide. Those charges may either be paid directly by the family or they can be assumed by the newly selected funeral home and incorporated into their own charges.

Miscommunication

In my experience, the majority of issues or problems that exist between consumers and funeral homes stem from a lack of communication. Often these problems are the failure on the part of one or both parties to manage expectations. The death of someone we love can be an overwhelming experience, which only heightens the potential for miscommunication.

When I was the executive director of Selected Independent Funeral Homes (SIFH), we required our funeral home members to send survey forms to the families they had served. One of the questions on the form was, "Would you recommend this funeral home to others?" Year after year, 99% of the responses received indicated the family was satisfied with the services that had been provided, and would recommend the funeral home to others.

When a family indicated they would not recommend the funeral home, it was my standard procedure to contact the owner of the funeral home and let him or her know we had received this response from a family they had served. I would encourage them to take steps necessary to find out exactly what went wrong, and what the funeral home could do to correct the problem. In nearly all instances, the funeral home owner would later report that the issue had been resolved. In all but a few cases over a period of more than ten years, the problem was simply caused by a lack of communication. Either something was not presented in a way that was clear to the family, or the funeral director wasn't aware that confusion existed. In any event, the families were usually satisfied with the result and no further action was necessary.

My first recommendation to people who are dissatisfied with a funeral home during the arrangement process is to express your concerns to the funeral director with whom you are working or, if necessary, the owner or manager of the funeral home. Speak with him about the issue and give him the opportunity to correct the problem. Many funeral homes have been in business for three or more generations, and they are eager to protect the reputations it has taken them so long to build. In all but the rarest of circumstances, they want to resolve the issue to whatever degree is necessary to satisfy the family.

If that approach fails, you have other options to resolve a dispute with a funeral home. Many funeral homes in the U.S., Canada, and abroad are members of the National Funeral Directors Association (nfda.org), which is the largest association in the industry. Other organizations, such as Selected Independent Funeral Homes (selectedfuneralhomes.org), Order of the Golden Rule (ogr.org), or state associations will often be willing to help. While these organizations don't have any regulatory authority, they can intercede on behalf of the consumer and serve as the mediator in attempts to arrive at some mutually acceptable resolution.

As a last resort, you have the option of contacting the regulatory authority in your state. Currently, the state of Colorado does not require licensure of funeral directors. But in all other states, if the conduct of the funeral home is a violation of the regulations, the licensing authority is empowered to take disciplinary action, which can ultimately result in the suspension or revocation of the funeral home's and/or funeral director's licenses.

If you think the funeral home may be in violation of the Federal Trade Commission's Funeral

Rule, you can contact the FTC. The Commission's website, ftc.gov, provides instructions for filing a complaint. I'll provide details of the Funeral Rule in the next chapter.

As part of its enforcement effort, the FTC periodically conducts compliance "sweeps" by sending undercover shoppers into funeral homes. Posing as people interested in making funeral arrangements, their goal is to determine whether the funeral home is complying with the rule by distributing General Price Lists and providing purchasers with required information.

A sweep by the FTC in 2012 found that, of the 127 funeral homes that were visited by the undercover shoppers, 23 of them (18%) failed to distribute a "General Price List" (GPL) as required by the Funeral Rule, or violated other sections of the Rule. In my opinion, failure to comply with the Funeral Rule, particularly on repeated occasions, is inexcusable. The Rule has been in existence for nearly thirty years, and complying with it is not complicated, burdensome, nor expensive. I don't understand why any funeral home would knowingly risk its reputation or civil penalties of $16,000 per violation by failing to train and monitor its employees to ensure compliance with the Funeral Rule. If you have a face-to-face discussion with a funeral director about funeral arrangements, and you don't receive a GPL early in the conversation, I suggest you ask for one, or perhaps choose another funeral home.

Dying Away From Home

It's not uncommon for people to die many miles away from home, either in their own country or abroad, and this presents some different but not insurmountable circumstances. If an American citizen dies in the U.S., but outside his or her home community or state, it's a very simple matter of having the remains transferred from the funeral home in the city or town where the death occurred to the one that will be handling the arrangements. For example, let's say I live in Illinois and I have a sister, who lives with my family and me. She has been plagued with heart disease for several years, and she has died in California while vacationing there. Under these circumstances, I would contact the local funeral home in Illinois that will be handling the funeral arrangements, and ask them to arrange for my sister's body to be sent back to Illinois. This course of action would most likely be more efficient and less expensive than it would be if I contacted the funeral home in California directly.

By communicating only with the receiving funeral home in Illinois, I need to work with only one funeral home. The funeral director can easily determine what funeral home in California currently has custody of the body or, if the body were in a hospital or a morgue or some other facility, what funeral home would be located near that facility. With only one or two phone calls, the Illinois funeral home can instruct the one in California to take custody of the body, prepare it for shipment, arrange for the shipping by commercial airline, and transport the body to the airport.

By following the process I've just described, it's possible for me to minimize the cost of the services provided by the California funeral home. Typically, when one funeral home is dealing directly with another, reduced prices may apply. For example, if the funeral home in California typically charges $500 for embalming, that is what I would pay if I contacted them directly. If, on the other hand, the California funeral home is providing "trade embalming" for the funeral home in Illinois, it could be done at a reduced rate, perhaps something on the order of $350. These policies will vary by funeral home, and it's important to discuss these options with the funeral director you have chosen.

In my example, the body will be transported to Illinois in an "air tray," a container that is specifically designed for this purpose. If I were going to be buying a casket, it would normally be sold to me by the funeral home in Illinois. If I had contacted the California funeral home directly, it's possible that they may have attempted to sell me a casket, although I wouldn't have been there to see various styles and compare prices. It's a practice that is frowned upon in the funeral industry. Typically, the funeral home that is handling the majority of the arrangements and services would also provide the casket.

Let's examine one variation of this scenario. My sister and I had discussed her preferences for her final arrangements, and we agreed that she would be cremated and a memorial service would be held at her favorite location in our community. When she died, neither my family members nor I felt the need to view her body prior to the cremation, so it would have made little sense to incur the expense to have her returned to Illinois. In that case, it probably would have been easier and more economical for me to contact the California funeral home directly, arrange for my sister to be cremated, and have the cremated remains returned to me via the U.S. Postal Service. At the time of this writing, FedEx, UPS and DHL do not accept cremated remains for shipment.

When a U.S. citizen dies in a foreign country, the process is essentially the same as I have just described, with a few potential differences. It may be necessary for the funeral director in the U.S. to ask for assistance from the American embassy or consulate in the country where the death occurred. In some circumstances, the return of the remains to the U.S. may be briefly delayed due to documentation requirements, customs clearance, or other considerations.

CHAPTER THREE

YOUR RIGHTS AS A CONSUMER

In 1963, author Jessica Mitford published a book entitled *The American Way of Death* that was very critical of the funeral industry. It alleged numerous instances of questionable practices and outrageous prices, and was one of the harshest assessments of the funeral industry ever published. The funeral industry has been the recipient of a lot of bad press over the years, but Mitford's book resulted in increased scrutiny by the federal government.

Following lengthy Congressional hearings about allegations of inappropriate business practices by funeral homes, the U.S. Federal Trade Commission issued its "Funeral Rule," which went into effect on April 30, 1984. It was designed primarily to provide consumers with a method for comparing the services and prices of funeral homes by virtue of a standardized "General Price List," or GPL.

The FTC requires 16 separate items to appear on the GPL. They are as follows:

1. Basic services of funeral director and staff.
2. Transfer of remains to funeral home.
3. Embalming.
4. Other preparation of the body.

5. Use of facilities and staff for viewing.
6. Use of facilities and staff for funeral ceremony.
7. Use of facilities and staff for memorial service.
8. Use of equipment and staff for graveside service.
9. A hearse.
10. A limousine.
11. A casket price list listing the range of prices of the caskets the funeral home offers.
12. A price list for outer burial containers the funeral home offers.
13. Forwarding of remains to another funeral home.
14. Receiving remains from another funeral home.
15. Direct cremation.
16. Immediate burial.

Any of these services that a funeral home provides must appear on its GPL. If the funeral home offers additional services, they may also be listed.

Another important element of the Funeral Rule is the manner in which the FTC requires funeral homes to distribute the GPL to consumers. The Rule mandates that the funeral director must provide a copy of the GPL any time a consumer inquires in person regarding funeral arrangements. If the conversation doesn't take place at the funeral home, the GPL still needs to be distributed any time there's a face-to-face conversation about funeral ceremonies, prices, or other aspects of the funeral home's services, regardless of where the conversation takes place. Funeral homes will usually require their employees to keep copies of this document in the company's vehicles, so it will be available for distribution at a residence or other location when they arrive to transfer the deceased.

Because of this very specific distribution requirement, it's possible for consumers to misinterpret the intentions and sensitivity of the funeral director. I'll share with you a story about someone who responded quite negatively to being presented the GPL during his initial discussion and consultation with me.

One day shortly after the Funeral Rule became effective, a man came to the funeral home I worked for and wanted to talk to someone about a member of his family that had been killed in a snowmobile accident. Although I asked him to take a seat, he was understandably quite agitated and remained standing, anxious to obtain the information he was seeking. I told him that we would help in any way we could, and I would answer all of his questions. I added that before our conversation could proceed any further, I was legally required to provide him with the General Price List. The man did not respond well to that, to say the least. He said, "I'm not interested in your price list. I just need to talk about what's happened and what I need to do for my family. I think it's totally inappropriate to talk about prices right now." He was offended and angry, but I calmly explained about the FTC rule and the regulatory requirement to provide him that information immediately upon the outset of our discussion. He eventually understood, and we proceeded with the steps that needed to be taken, but the situation raised his stress level and caused a few moments of discomfort for us both.

Please try to remember this example when you are presented with a GPL early in the conversation with the funeral director. He or she is merely trying to comply with the FTC Rule, and those efforts should not be seen as demonstrating a lack of compassion, an inappropriate emphasis on money, or a sign of insensitivity to your loss.

The FTC also requires that consumers be able to obtain price information by telephone, simply by calling the funeral home and asking about the cost of various goods and services.

In addition to the 16 items that must appear on the GPL, there are also several disclosures the FTC requires. The disclosures must appear exactly as written by the FTC.

The first required disclosure on the GPL must include the effective date of the GPL, and is intended to inform purchasers that they may choose only those items they want to purchase, subject to specific requirements, if any, that must be disclosed by the funeral home:

> *These prices are effective as of [date].*
>
> *The goods and services shown below are those we can provide to our customers. You may choose only the items you desire. However, any funeral arrangements you select will include a charge for our basic services and overhead. If legal or other requirements mean you must buy any items you did not specifically ask for, we*

will explain the reason in writing on the statement we provide describing the funeral goods and services you selected.

The purchasers must also be informed that embalming is not generally required by law, and the family usually has the right to choose a type of arrangement that does not require embalming, such as a viewing with a closed casket. Funeral homes must include the following disclaimer on the GPL:

Except in certain special cases, embalming is not required by law. Embalming may be necessary, however, if you select certain funeral arrangements, such as a funeral with viewing. If you do not want embalming, you usually have the right to choose an arrangement that does not require you to pay for it, such as direct cremation or immediate burial.

It's important to remember, however, that a funeral home may require that embalming be performed if the arrangements include a public visitation (wake) or funeral ceremony with an open casket.

Basic Services of Funeral Director and Staff

One of the first items on the General Price List is the "Basic Services of Funeral Director and Staff." In the terminology used by the FTC, this item is the only one on the GPL deemed to be "non-declinable," which means it's the one fee that applies to virtually every type of arrangement the funeral home is equipped to handle. Depending on the type of arrangements, either the total fee or a portion of it will apply, and the purchaser doesn't have the option of deleting it, as he would other services and related fees, such as embalming. The required disclosure for this item is:

> *Our services include: conducting the arrangements conference; planning the funeral; consulting with family and clergy; shelter of remains; preparing and filing of necessary notices; obtaining necessary authorizations and permits; coordinating with the cemetery, crematory, or other third parties. In addition, this fee includes a proportionate share of our basic overhead costs.*
>
> *This fee for our basic services and overhead will be added to the total cost of the funeral arrangements you select. (This fee is already included in our charges for direct cremations, immediate burials, and forwarding or receiving remains.)*

Caskets and Outer Burial Containers

The FTC requires the funeral home to include on its Casket Price List all the caskets and alternative containers it normally offers for sale; the number of which will vary at different funeral homes. Some may offer as few as eight or ten caskets for purchase, while others may offer 20 or more; what they stock is simply a decision made by the funeral home's management.

The same requirement applies for the Outer Burial Container Price List. All of the burial vaults the funeral home would normally make available must appear on the list.

I am not aware of any state or local law that requires an outer burial container. However, many cemeteries do require some sort of outer enclosure, commonly known as a grave liner or a burial vault, to make it easier to maintain the cemetery grounds. If a casket is buried and deteriorates over a period of years, the ground is likely to settle, which will require the cemetery to fill in the surface of that gravesite, perhaps repeatedly. An outer burial container supports the weight of the earth above it. To clarify this point, the FTC requires the following disclosure to appear on the Statement of Funeral Good and Services Selected, which I explain later in this chapter:

> *In most areas of the country, state or local law does not require that you buy a container to surround the casket in the grave. However, many cemeteries require that you have such a container so that the grave will not sink in. Either a grave liner or a burial vault will satisfy these requirements.*

Direct Cremation or Immediate Burial

The FTC views alternatives to the traditional funeral, such as direct cremation or immediate burial, as separate items that are presented as a "package." These terms are generally used to describe the cremation or burial of the body as soon as possible after death, which may or may not be followed by a memorial service or other tribute.

These packages, if offered by the funeral home, must appear on the GPL and include a description of the items contained in the package, including the basic services of the funeral director and staff, initial transfer from the place of death to the funeral home and/or cremation facility or cemetery, crematory or cemetery fees, and an "alternative container" for the cremation or casket for immediate burial.

The alternative container can be provided by the funeral home or by the family, must be rigid enough to permit the transfer of the body to the crematory, and will be cremated along with the body. In the interest of ensuring that consumers understand their options for direct cremation, the following disclosure must appear on the GPL:

> *"If you want to arrange a direct cremation, you can use an alternative container. Alternative containers encase the body and can be made of materials like fiberboard or composition materials (with or without an outside covering). The containers we provide are (specify containers)."*

The GPL must specify the price of the direct cremation or immediate burial if the casket or alternative container is purchased from the funeral home, as well as the price if the family provides an alternative container.

Statement of Funeral Goods and Services

The Funeral Rule also requires the funeral home to provide the purchaser with a document called the Statement of Funeral Goods and Services Selected (SFGSS) when the arrangements have been finalized. On that document, each of items the family has chosen will appear, along with the prices of those items. That document must be provided to the family and signed by the responsible party before any money is paid to the funeral home.

The following disclosures are required to appear on this document:

> *Charges are only for those items that you selected or that are required. If we are required by law or by a cemetery or crematory to use any items, we will explain the reasons in writing below.*
>
> *If you selected a funeral that may require embalming, such as a funeral with viewing, you may have to pay for embalming. You do not have to pay for embalming you did not approve if you selected arrangements such as a direct cremation or immediate burial. If we charged for embalming, we will explain why below.*

An Important Note

While the stated intent of the FTC Funeral Rule was to protect consumers by providing a method by which to compare services and prices offered by different and often competing funeral homes, the Commission did not expand its regulatory scope to cemeteries. In my opinion, the failure to include cemeteries in the regulations could put consumers at a disadvantage.

In the past few years, more cemeteries have begun to sell funeral-related products that had previously been available almost exclusively from funeral homes. These items include caskets, vaults, and cremation urns, among others. One might ask why cemeteries are not required to comply with the Funeral Rule if they are selling the very same products as the funeral homes. The answer lies in the wording of the Funeral Rule, which states, "All 'funeral providers' must comply with the Rule. You are a funeral provider if you sell or offer to sell *both* funeral goods *and* funeral services to the public."

I have emphasized the words "both" and "and" in the paragraph above, because those words are critical in this context. It's on that basis that cemeteries have fought vigorously to remain outside the scope of the funeral rule, claiming that while they may sell funeral goods such as caskets, they don't provide funeral services. They further state that because of that distinction, they don't engage in the sale of "funeral goods *and* services," and are therefore exempt from the Rule.

Many in the funeral profession feel this is a distinction without a difference. In reality, many cemeteries now have chapels or other facilities they provide for family members and friends to gather for a brief committal service prior to the actual burial or cremation, and it could be argued by doing so they are providing "funeral services."

In my role as executive director of SIFH (known then as National Selected Morticians, or NSM) I participated in a public workshop conducted in 1999 by the FTC as part of its review of the Funeral Rule. In preparation for that event, NSM enlisted the expertise of a noted economist and former FTC staff member to offer his expert opinion that cemeteries should be required to comply with the Funeral Rule. We advocated that the language of the Rule be amended to read "funeral goods *or* services." We presented compelling information that the revision was necessary because if consumers were presumably at risk when purchasing funeral goods or services from funeral homes, it follows they are at risk when purchasing those goods and services from any provider. Unfortunately, the FTC staff did not find the revision necessary, and this section of the Rule has not yet been amended.

Many cemeteries will require family members of the deceased to personally visit the cemetery office prior to the burial to confirm the location of the cemetery lot and sign an "interment order." This is a valid request, but it has been reported that during these meetings, personnel from some cemeteries may also attempt to sell the family a casket, burial vault, cremation urn, or other item, even when the family has already purchased the item(s) from the funeral home, claiming that they can be purchased from the cemetery at a lower price. While the claims of lower prices may or may not be true, family members should be careful to obtain all the facts before making these purchase decisions, and should not allow themselves to be pressured into making decisions without enough time to consider the results.

In addition to the Funeral Rule, funeral homes are regulated at the state level. At the time of this writing, Colorado is the only state in the United States that does not require a funeral director to be licensed. All other states require the funeral director and the establishment itself to be licensed by the state, although the specific requirements for licensure vary.

The regulatory board or agency that issues the licenses is also charged with compliance enforcement. If a consumer feels there has been a case of fraud or other act by the funeral home that may be a violation of the state regulations, there is a process by which a complaint can be filed with the appropriate regulatory agency. The complaint process can take several forms, but the idea is to make the regulatory board aware of the alleged violation, render an opinion on the issue, and if appropriate, take disciplinary action against the licensee, which may result in the suspension or revocation of the license(s). In my experience, these regulatory agencies are composed of representatives of the funeral industry, state employees, and one or two members of the general public (usually appointed by the governor). In an effort to provide them with a balanced perspective as they address alleged violations.

Chapter Four

When a Death Occurs

When someone dies, regardless of the location, there is the need for an authorized person to formally make the pronouncement of death and complete a death certificate. Generally, if the person has been under the direct care of an attending physician, the pronouncement and death certificate will be that physician's responsibility.

In some states, if the attending physician isn't available to carry out those duties, the responsibility can fall to a registered nurse, who can complete the pronouncement and issue a preliminary certificate. The final death certificate will be completed by the attending physician at the time he or she is available. In some states, the death certificate must be signed before the body can legally be removed from the place of death.

If the death is the result of an accident, suicide, or homicide, or in those cases when the cause of death cannot be easily determined, a coroner or medical examiner is notified. He or she will usually go to the scene where the death has occurred (or authorize a representative to do so) to review the circumstances surrounding the death, and will then have the body transported to the medical examiner's office or to a funeral home, depending upon the circumstances and the procedure in effect in that jurisdiction.

It is also common for the local police to respond to calls for emergency medical services or reports of an unexpected death. I have a friend whose mother died, unexpectedly yet peacefully, at home in her sleep. He later told me he was quite surprised when, in addition to the emergency medical personnel that responded to his call, a police officer arrived and remained there until after the medical examiner had come and gone. In my experience, it's not unusual for law enforcement officials to secure the place of death until the medical examiner determines whether further investigation is necessary, but it can be unsettling for family members.

As part of an investigation into a death, the medical examiner may order an autopsy. This is a routine but detailed investigative procedure, performed by a forensic pathologist, during which toxicological samples of blood, urine, and other body fluids are collected. A full examination of the external aspects of the body and the internal organs is conducted in an effort to determine the exact cause and manner of death. This procedure will sometimes delay the release of the body to the funeral home, although medical examiners and pathologists do their best to minimize the time it takes to complete their investigations. Typically, an autopsy will not in any way alter the family's ability to view the deceased, if they choose to do so, or to have an open casket for a viewing or visitation. Although there may be some extensive incisions made for the purpose of examining the internal organs, a qualified embalmer is capable of minimizing their appearance.

There is a distinction between autopsies ordered by a medical examiner, and autopsies for which hospitals or physicians ask permission from the deceased's next of kin. The former is a legal necessity and the family has no authority to prevent the autopsy from being performed. In the latter case, the family usually has the right to deny permission for the autopsy to be conducted.

Notifying the Funeral Home

When a death occurs, and arrangements have not been planned in advance, those responsible for the funeral arrangements may feel pressured into making decisions quickly. If the death is unexpected, the feeling of urgency may be even greater, because it's unlikely that family members have considered the responsibilities and options facing them. When these decisions are made without enough time to think them through and consider alternatives, the potential for anxiety, confusion, and regret can be increased.

In most cases, you should try to resist the urge to make decisions quickly, and take whatever time is necessary to finalize funeral arrangements that incorporate your spiritual, cultural, emotional, and economic needs. Some religious denominations require burial or cremation of the deceased within a specific period of time following the death, but in the absence of those requirements, there is generally no need for decisions about funeral arrangements to be influenced by time pressure.

If you have selected a funeral home, contact them and provide them with the name and location of the deceased, as well as your name, contact information and your relationship to the person who has died. It's also common during this call to schedule an appointment with the funeral director to discuss the arrangements. It is normally the responsibility of the funeral home to determine whether the pronouncement of death has been completed, if the death certificate has been signed, and when the body will be available for transfer to their facility.

If the person died in his or her home or other residential location, and if you or other family members want to spend time in the presence of the body before it is transferred to the funeral home, I suggest that you notify the funeral home to advise them of the death and establish a time for them to arrive, or let them know that you will call them when the time is appropriate.

During this initial telephone conversation, the funeral director may ask if the deceased is to be embalmed. In the next chapter, I will explain the process of embalming and offer some practical considerations upon which to base your answer.

The Death Certificate

There are several pieces of information required for the death certificate, including the full name of the deceased, date of birth, place of birth, and parent's names. It's not unusual to see questions regarding the ethnicity of the deceased (Hispanic, African American, Asian, etc.), the number of years of education, marital status and the name of the most recent spouse. If the spouse is a woman, her maiden name (if applicable) would be required on the death certificate. Other information includes occupation of the deceased (or his or her line of work prior to retirement, if applicable), and the type of business or industry. If the deceased was a veteran, the death certificate requires details about military service, which can be obtained from the military discharge document (known as form DD214) that was issued at the time the person was separated from military duty.

Additional information to be completed by the attending physician or medical examiner and the funeral director includes the date and place of burial, the name of the cemetery, the name of the funeral home, and the name and license number of the funeral director handling the arrangements.

Obituaries and Death Notices

Usually, families choose to publish an announcement in one or more newspapers to notify others of a death and provide details regarding the funeral or memorial service. There may be two different forms of notification appearing in various newspapers, depending upon their policy. Some newspapers will print what is formally called a death notice, which is an abbreviated notification of the death, containing the name of the deceased, the date of death, a list of surviving family members, details about the funeral arrangements, and place of burial. Newspapers charge for these notices, usually on a per line basis. Death notices can be quite expensive, and families often try to minimize the information included in order to control the cost of publication. Some newspapers will place some restrictions on the length of the death notice, particularly in large, metropolitan areas, primarily out of concern for the space available within a particular edition of the newspaper. Most often, families can specify the number of days the notice will be printed, and will be charged for each time it's published.

In place of, or in addition to the death notice, most newspapers will print an obituary, which is often considered by the newspaper to be a news item. As such, the newspaper retains editorial control over the content. They will determine what is appropriate for inclusion in the obituary, and when it will appear, and will usually print it only once. In the past, newspapers would assign responsibility for obituary writing to one or more staff reporters. Today, however, family members may be required to write the obituary, which may result in spelling or grammatical errors. I recommend asking a trusted relative or friend to proofread the obituary before it is submitted to the newspaper.

Deciding what information to include in the obituary is something that can be made easier by advance planning and discussion among family members. The obituary is designed to create a biographical summary of the life of the deceased, and includes the following: birthplace; education; various aspects of the person's career; personal interests; and the names of family members and an announcement of the funeral arrangements. As one might expect, families want to have the obituary or death notice appear in the newspaper as soon as possible after the death has occurred to provide people with enough notice to be able to plan to attend ceremonies.

In recent years, companies have emerged that enable funeral homes and/or families to submit information to obituary websites. An example of these websites is tributes.com. Many newspapers have opted to use these companies that, for a fee, will host their death notices and obituaries online, making them accessible outside the paper's immediate market area.

Some of these companies permit families to add printed information, a video tribute, and an online guest book. People reading the obituary in the paper or online will be directed to a link that will enable them to sign a virtual guest book and leave words of condolence to the family. It's an option that is likely to become more popular, and people need to be aware of the additional benefits that Internet-based obituaries offer over the traditional printed versions.

Clothing

If there is going to be a viewing or ceremony with an open casket, clothing must be provided for the deceased. Even if the deceased will not be viewed by the family prior to the final disposition, it's not uncommon for the funeral home to ask the family to provide clothing. The clothing should be chosen by the family as appropriate for the character and preferences of the deceased—what they would normally wear—and should include any other items that the person would normally have worn. Shoes are not necessary, but may be included at the family's discretion.

Chapter Five

Understand the Details & Consider Your Alternatives

In this chapter, I'll explain some of the aspects of funeral planning that most people don't really understand, the details you need, and alternatives you may wish to consider when planning a tribute.

Embalming

One of the topics I have been most frequently asked about — by friends, acquaintances, and children at various presentations I've made to schools — is embalming. It has often been my sense that, while they're not sure they really want to know, they have an undeniable curiosity about it.

Embalming is more common in North America than it is in other parts of the world. It first gained wide acceptance in the U.S. during the time of the Civil War, when there was a desperate need to develop a method to preserve the remains of the soldiers killed in battle so they could be transported back to their homes for their funerals.

Under the FTC Funeral Rule, consumers in the U.S. usually have the right to choose funeral arrangements that don't require embalming. If there are circumstances that invoke a legal requirement that the body be embalmed, which is very rare, the funeral home must disclose that fact to the family. For example, some states may require that a body be embalmed if the burial or cremation is not performed within a specified period of time following the death, and if refrigeration is not available.

On a more practical level, funeral homes will typically require that a body be embalmed if it's going to be publicly displayed in an open casket. If the casket is going to be closed, or there is viewing only by the family, embalming will usually not be necessary.

At the time of the first contact between the family and the funeral home, it's common for the funeral director to ask the family if they want to have the body embalmed. As part of this discussion, the funeral director should explain the reason for the question and describe the options available to the family. Most often, the funeral director is asking the question because it's advantageous to begin the embalming process as soon as practical after the death, and it's generally easier to obtain the desired results before decomposition begins.

The family shouldn't feel pressured into answering the question immediately. If there is any doubt about the type of arrangements they prefer, they should feel comfortable in postponing the decision. Most funeral homes now have refrigeration facilities, much like a morgue in a hospital, where the body will be kept to delay the onset of decomposition, and still permit embalming within a reasonable period of time. On the other hand, if the family believes there is a possibility that the arrangements will include an open casket, they may wish to give permission for embalming in order to keep that option available.

So, what exactly is embalming, and why is it necessary in some circumstances? Embalming serves one primary purpose: temporary preservation of the body. Decomposition can start fairly quickly following death, and its progress is subject to physiological and environmental conditions. When a death occurs in a warmer climate, the decomposition can be more rapid. Other contributing factors are the weight of the person, the cause of death, and medication the person was taking. The same factors apply to the embalming process and can have some influence on the effectiveness of the embalming chemicals used.

I will not attempt to describe the entire embalming process, but for our purposes here, the best analogy I can offer is that it's similar in concept to a blood transfusion. A formaldehyde-based preservative chemical is injected, under pressure, through an artery, into the circulatory system of the body. (In 1987, the U.S. Environmental Protection Agency [EPA] designated formaldehyde as a potential cancer-causing agent. Alternative preservative chemicals are available.) The circulatory system can be seen as a closed system with a maximum capacity, so when fluid is injected through the artery and allowed to circulate through the body, the blood is displaced, and exits the body through a vein.

In addition to the arterial embalming I have just described, it's also necessary for the embalmer to remove the blood and other bodily fluids from the chest cavity and the abdomen, particularly in the hollow organs, by use of a large needle called a "trocar." It's attached to a suction device, an "aspirator," to evacuate the fluids from the cavities. Once aspiration is completed and most of the fluids have been removed from the thoracic and abdominal cavities, a preservative solution, again usually formaldehyde-based, is injected through that same needle back into the cavity. That procedure is intended to preserve the internal organs for a period long enough for the public viewing and visitation and funeral.

It's important for people to understand that although there have been some remains that have been preserved for many, many years, embalming is not in any way permanent. The Egyptians are the first known civilization to have practiced a form of embalming, and while they had developed that science to a point where it produced quite remarkable results in terms of long-term preservation, it also resulted in mummification, which is the removal of all fluid from the tissue. When all the moisture is removed, any decomposition that takes place does so very slowly. Modern embalming procedures do not remove all moisture from the body, and despite the best embalming, decomposition will progress. For those that choose to authorize the embalming process, please realize that any claims or promises made that it will preserve the body indefinitely are simply not true.

Methods of Final Disposition

Earth Burial

Currently, the most prevalent method of final disposition in the United States is traditional burial in a grave in a cemetery. Many people own cemetery lots in the communities in which they live, or have a grave reserved for them in the family lot purchased by their parents or other ancestors.

A cemetery lot can contain a single grave or multiple graves. In some areas, graves may be designated as "double depth," which means at the time of the first burial in that grave, it will be dug deep enough to accommodate two burials, one above the other. In my experience, burials in most cemeteries are single depth.

When a death occurs, if a death is imminent, or when someone is interested in planning in advance, it will be necessary to determine what cemetery space is available. If the person already owns a cemetery lot, the person responsible for the arrangements will need to produce the deed for the cemetery lot or grave. The deed will provide proof of ownership, and identify the location of the grave within the cemetery. If the deed is not available, it's usually possible to contact the cemetery and ask them to research their records to determine ownership and whether graves are still available for burial. Once that information has been verified, the cemetery will arrange for the grave to be opened when necessary.

If the family does not have cemetery space, they will need to purchase it. The prices for cemetery spaces can vary significantly. Some cemeteries are established as for-profit entities, while others are owned by not-for - profit associations or trusts. The cost of cemetery property can range from several hundred to many thousands of dollars, depending upon the cemetery's location and desirability and the number of grave spaces contained within the lot.

A portion of the money paid to purchase cemetery property is usually designated for deposit in the cemetery's perpetual care fund. This is money set aside, usually in a trust, to provide for the ongoing maintenance of the cemetery space, hopefully indefinitely. Because of the ongoing nature of the cemetery's maintenance requirements, it's important for owners and prospective owners of cemetery property to understand how the fund is administered. If the monies are in a trust, who are the trustees and how is the money invested? If the funds are mismanaged, how will deficiencies in the fund be compensated for? What guarantee does the purchaser/owner have that the cemetery will be appropriately cared for in the near and distant future? These are important questions, because perpetual care funds can be exhausted due to poor management, leaving cemeteries to neglect and disrepair.

In addition to the purchase of the cemetery lot itself, there is the cost of preparing, or "opening" the grave for the burial. This amount can range from several hundred dollars to a thousand dollars or more. When a death occurs, the funeral director will contact the cemetery and arrange for the grave to be opened, and will provide the family with the specific charges for the cemetery services. The charges can vary not only by cemetery, but also according to the day and time of the burial. Cemeteries often apply additional charges if the burial is going to take place on a weekend or holiday.

A common cemetery requirement is for the casket to be enclosed in some kind of rigid container, referred to by the FTC as an “Outer Burial Container.” As mentioned previously, a grave liner or vault is required by the cemetery is to support the weight of the soil above the casket, as the decomposition of the casket and the body takes place over a period of years. The grave liner is the simplest form of outer burial enclosure. It is usually the minimum required by the cemetery, and is constructed of a solid concrete base, approximately an inch and a half or two inches thick. A concrete cover is placed on the top of the grave liner after the casket is lowered into it.

An alternative to a grave liner is a burial vault, which essentially serves the same purpose as a grave liner, but is constructed of thicker concrete, perhaps 3 to 4 inches or more. The primary difference between grave liners and burial vaults is that the latter are advertised by the manufacturers and funeral homes as being either water resistant or waterproof. For some people, that's an important consideration. They find comfort in the fact that this burial vault is designed, and in some instances, warrantied by the manufacturer to prevent the entrance of water or other gravesite related substances into the vault itself. For others, the notion of a waterproof burial vault is seen as an unnecessary and perhaps nonsensical expense.

Many people will ask how they will ever know if the vault is really preventing water from getting into it. The answer is that they won't know, unless for some reason it becomes necessary to move, or "disinter" the vault. Some families will choose, at some time in the future, to relocate to another community, and will disinter the vault containing the casket and body, and move it to another cemetery. If, upon disinterment, the vault is found to have failed to prevent the entry of water during the warranty period, the funeral home and the vault company will provide a new vault for installation in the grave at the cemetery where the remains will be reburied.

Burial vaults can be significantly more expensive than grave liners. At minimum, the vaults are lined with a type of plastic liner to provide the waterproofing, but they may also be lined with steel, copper, or bronze. Regardless of the materials used in the construction of the vault, it's important to point out that none of them will in any way prevent the eventual decomposition of the body or the casket.

One recent variation of traditional earth burial is the practice of "green burial." A green burial cemetery, out of concern for the environmental impact some interment-related materials may have on the cemetery and surrounding area, places restrictions on various aspects of the burial itself, such as requiring that the body not be embalmed with formaldehyde or any other toxic chemicals. Cemetery rules will also mandate that the casket, or alternative container, or shroud (a simple cloth in which the body is wrapped) containing the body be made of biodegradable substances, and will prohibit the use of any outer burial enclosures. The goal is to take steps to ensure the preservation of the environment and to prevent the introduction of any substances into the cemetery that would be ecologically harmful. There are varying standards set by different green burial organizations.

One of the first organizations to research and adopt ways in which to develop and promote green burials is the Green Burial Council (You can find their website at www.greenburialcouncil.org). On the website, there is information about green burial standards, the history of the organization, some frequently asked questions and misconceptions about green burial, and assistance with finding a cemetery and/or funeral home that can help families considering this option.

Cremation

Cremation has been widely used in other parts of the world for generations, and it has become an increasingly popular alternative to traditional earth burial in North America. Simply defined, cremation is the reduction of the body to bone fragments by the use of intense heat. Crematories are often contained within cemeteries, but they may also be small, stand-alone facilities. Some funeral homes house cremation equipment, the main component being the cremation chamber, or "retort." As cremation rates have risen, more funeral homes have purchased this equipment, enabling them to provide cremation services directly to families without the need to rely on third-party crematories.

In some states, regulations prohibit funeral homes from operating crematories, and /or prohibit crematories from operating funeral homes within the confines of their property. These regulations are viewed as archaic by many, and will likely be subject to increased scrutiny and revision in the future as cremation continues to become more popular.

Currently in the United States, cremation is the method of disposition for approximately 40% of all deaths, although that percentage varies by region and state. It's generally acknowledged that cremation is most prevalent on the coasts and much less common in parts of the Midwest, where people tend to be more traditional in their approach to funeral arrangements. Information published by the Cremation Association of North America, (you can find their website at: cremationassociation.org) predicts that by 2025, the cremation rate in the United States will be well above 50%.

One question often asked is whether cremation is less expensive than burial. The simple answer is maybe. Cremation doesn't necessarily require the purchase of cemetery space, or the expenses of grave preparation, or a casket and outer burial container. However, there are variables and choices available that can lower the cost of burial and, conversely, increase the cost of cremation.

There are a few other things you need to know about cremation. First, there is a misconception among some that when cremation is the chosen form of final disposition, it is not possible to have a traditional visitation or funeral. That is certainly not true. Burial and cremation are simply different methods of disposition, and nothing more. If one chooses cremation as the method of disposition, it's still possible for the body to be embalmed, prepared for visitation, and be present during a funeral service.

Some states require a waiting period between the time the death occurs and the time the cremation can take place. The state in which I worked had a 48-hour waiting period, which meant, for example, if a death occurred at noon on Tuesday, the body couldn't be cremated until after noon on Thursday. The primary reason for this requirement is the need to ensure that the cause of death had been determined beyond any reasonable doubt. If a body is buried and questions arise in the following days, or weeks, or months as to the cause or manner of death, the body can be exhumed and further examined. Obviously, the cremation process is irreversible, and once the cremation has taken place, further examination of the remains is no longer possible.

The waiting period will vary from state to state, and some may not require any waiting period. But people need to be aware when they're planning for final disposition that a required waiting period may have an effect on how soon after death the cremated remains will be available to them.

Many states require that, in addition to the death certificate, a medical examiner's authorization for cremation must be obtained prior to the cremation. This requirement is an additional step to ensure that no further inquiry into the cause of death in necessary.

As discussed earlier in this guide, crematories normally require that the body be transported to them in a rigid container. Requirements may vary, but the minimum acceptable container would be made of cardboard, with a particleboard or plywood base, so it can be lifted as necessary. The FTC acknowledges this requirement and specifies that families choosing cremation have the right to use an alternative container, which can either be purchased from the funeral home or provided by the family themselves, as long as it is a container that meets the specifications of the crematory.

If the deceased has a pacemaker that was surgically implanted, part of the cremation authorization will disclose to you that the pacemaker will be removed prior to the cremation itself and request your permission for that procedure. This is because pacemakers, when exposed to the high temperatures attained in the cremation process, can explode and do severe damage to the inner linings of the cremation chamber.

Family members should advise the funeral home of any jewelry that the deceased was wearing at the time of death, and specify whether it should be removed prior to the cremation. Depending on the type of material used in the jewelry, it may or may not be incinerated during the cremation process.

Many funeral homes and crematories require positive identification of the deceased by the next of kin before the cremation takes place. This is especially true if the death occurred in a hospital or nursing home or other facility rather than at the residence of the deceased, where there would be family members present at the time the deceased is transferred to the funeral home.

The identification can be done at the funeral home in a setting where the body can be viewed, either in a casket (if one has been selected), in an alternative cremation container, or on a table (with the body covered by a sheet or clothing if the family has provided it). The legally responsible next of kin will be asked to positively identify the deceased, and verification of the identification may be included in the cremation authorization form. Under normal circumstances, the family should not expect to pay additional fees for this identification process.

If you choose to have a funeral service with the body present prior to the cremation, or prefer a casket rather than an alternative container, the casket typically needs to be made of wood. If there are any pieces of metal involved in the construction of the casket, they will remain following the cremation process, and those metal remnants will be removed before the remains are processed and given to the family for disposition.

While cremation is a method of disposition, in the strictest sense, it's not truly the final component of disposition. At the conclusion of the cremation process, the personnel supervising the cremation process remove the bone fragments that remain in the retort. Because these fragments can be fairly large, they are processed in a machine specifically designed for that purpose, which reduces them to a more granular consistency. The granules are what people normally refer to as "ashes," although some people use the terms "cremated remains" or "cremains." If people choose to scatter the ashes themselves it's important for them to be prepared for the fact that what they will be seeing upon opening that container is not ash as one would normally envision it, like the ashes that remain in a fireplace. They're much coarser, and people can be quite shocked upon opening the container and seeing the contents.

I recommend to those choosing cremation that they consider, discuss, and ultimately decide upon a final disposition of the cremated remains, and take the necessary action as soon as practical after the cremation has taken place. I know there are funeral homes that have closets or rooms that hold many, many, containers of unclaimed cremated remains. In those instances, the family arranged for the cremation with full knowledge that after the cremation, they would need to make decisions about what was to be done with the ashes, and, for a variety of reasons, they procrastinated, and years went by. The funeral home was ultimately left with the need to contact the next of kin, if possible, to determine what was to be done with the cremated remains. In some cases, their attempts were unsuccessful or went unacknowledged. This situation presents a potentially enormous liability issue for the funeral home or crematory that has custody of the remains, and many funeral homes will no longer agree to hold them beyond a brief period of time following the cremation.

There are several options from which people can choose for the ultimate disposition of cremated remains. They can be buried in a cemetery, in an existing grave where someone is buried (subject to the cemetery's policy), in a portion of a vacant grave, or in a section of the cemetery specifically designated for the purpose.

Some cemeteries and houses of worship contain a "columbarium," an aboveground structure built specifically for the placement of cremated remains. The individual spaces within the columbarium are referred to as "niches."

After the cremated remains are removed from the retort and processed, they are placed in what crematories and funeral homes commonly refer to as a "temporary container," which can be made of plastic, aluminum, or cardboard with a plastic liner. While this temporary container may be acceptable for some columbaria and cemeteries, others will require the family to provide a cremation urn, a more rigid and permanent container for the cremated remains. Urns can be made of various materials, including wood, metal, or substances that have the appearance of marble or granite. There are also temporary urns for scattering the remains in the ocean or other body of water. After being submerged, the urn dissolves and releases the contents, preventing them from being carried away by the wind.

Keep in mind that unless cemetery or columbarium policy requires a cremation urn, it's not usually necessary to purchase one. If you prefer to use an urn, you can buy one from a funeral home, crematory, or other source, including online retailers. As an alternative to purchasing an urn, some people use a ceramic jar, vase, or other container that has special meaning for them. It's important, however, to ensure that the container you choose is large enough to accommodate the cremated remains. The funeral home or crematory staff can advise you on the necessary capacity of the container, and will usually have no objection to transferring the remains into the one you have provided.

If you opt to scatter the cremated remains, you are free to do so, within some basic guidelines. The primary restriction is that the cremated remains cannot be scattered on private property. I've known people that arranged for cremated remains to be scattered from an airplane over a favorite beach or lake. Others have secretly taken a portion of the cremated remains to the deceased's favorite golf course and scattered little bits of those remains among the greens and fairways, an option that I don't recommend. For obvious reasons, the people that maintain the golf courses frown upon such activity. The general recommendation is that people should not attempt to scatter cremated remains on the property of others without the property owner's permission. Funeral directors, crematory personnel, or state regulatory agencies can provide guidance on the permissible options.

As another alternative, some people will choose to transfer the cremated remains to an urn or other container they have chosen and will simply keep it at home in an area that is meaningful for them. They may be comforted by its presence, and will perhaps never feel it necessary to arrange for a more permanent location.

Entombment

Entombment is the placement of a casket in an aboveground structure called a mausoleum. Each individual space in the mausoleum, that will hold one casket, is known as a crypt. Mausoleums are typically located on the grounds of a cemetery. The front of the crypt is engraved with the name of the deceased, dates of birth and death, and other information as the owner or surviving family members prefer.

Alkaline Hydrolysis

There is a method of final disposition known as "alkaline hydrolysis" that has been introduced within the past few years. It hasn't yet been widely implemented, but has the potential to become more common. In this process, the body is placed into a specifically designed container and immersed in a solution of water and lye. The solution is heated and pressurized, and accelerates the decomposition that would ultimately take place under natural conditions. Although this method has only recently been used for the disposition of human remains, veterinary schools and other research facilities have relied upon it for many years.

The proponents of alkaline hydrolysis claim it's a more environmentally friendly alternative to cremation. It doesn't require the use of large quantities of fossil fuels, nor doesn't it result in pollutants being emitted into the atmosphere. It does not require the use of any type of alternative container or casket other than what is necessary to transport the remains to the facility. At the conclusion of the process, which takes several hours, all that is left are bone fragments, similar to those produced by cremation, which are collected, processed, and presented to the family for final disposition in essentially the same way cremated remains would be. The liquid solution that remains is ecologically benign, so it can simply be flushed into the normal waste stream.

It's an option that some states are currently struggling with. Regulatory agencies have been confronted by funeral home owners that want to make this option available to their customers, but because the regulatory agencies are not familiar with the process, there have been instances where it's been banned in some states, only to be reconsidered once more information comes to light. I suspect that while there are only a handful of funeral homes currently offering this option, it will become more prevalent.

Organ and Tissue Donation and Anatomical Gifts

According to the Revised Uniform Anatomical Gift Act (2009), an anatomical gift is defined as "a donation of one's organs or entire body for the purposes of transplantation, therapy, research, or education." It's intended to address the critical shortage of donated organs that currently exists.

Although the Act is meant to apply to all anatomical gifts, for the purposes of this guide, there are differences between organ and tissue donations for transplantation and whole body donations for education and research that deserve explanation.

Organ and Tissue Donation

Most people have some idea of what organ and tissue donation is and the desperate need for donated organs in the U.S and in other places around the world. Those considering donation often have questions regarding the restrictions the donation may impose on funeral arrangements. The simple answer is that the decision to donate organs will not usually have an effect on the ability of the family to arrange whatever type of funeral or disposition they choose. There may be some circumstances, however, when there may be a delay between the time when the death occurs and the time the body is released to the funeral home or other provider for funeral services and disposition.

The process of removing the organs from the body, known as "procurement," is usually performed in a surgical setting, depending on the organs that have been donated. After the death, surgical teams will be called in to procure the organs from the body, which can include the heart, liver, kidneys, skin, bones, and eyes.

As determined by a variety of factors, the organs may be used for transplantation or research.

When the procurement process is complete, the body will be released to the funeral home and the arrangements can proceed. If the family chooses arrangements that include an open casket, which usually requires embalming, it's the embalmer's responsibility to ensure that there are no visible indications that the donation has occurred.

Anatomical Gift for Research

In the case of a whole body donation, the body is donated to a medical school or other research facility for the purposes of research and education. This option does have an impact on the arrangements that may be available to the family members.

Medical schools will have the final authority to determine whether a body is acceptable for donation. The decision is based upon a number of factors, such as the age of the deceased, the cause of death, the condition of the body, and the amount of time that has elapsed since the time of death.

If the medical school declines the donation, it will be up to the family to arrange for a funeral or disposition. If the medical school accepts the donation, they will require the body be transported to them, unembalmed, and usually within a 24- to 48-hour period following the death.

Normally, a funeral home will be required to transport the body from the place of death to the medical school. The family has the option of arranging a memorial service any time after the death. It is usually difficult to arrange a funeral ceremony within the period of time in which the medical school must receive the body

It's not unusual for the medical school's research to take a year or more. At the time the body is donated, the family will be required to decide what is to happen to the body once the medical school is ready to release it. Depending upon the medical school's policy, the family may have the option of being notified when the research is completed and the remains are available. The family will then retain a funeral home to transfer the remains from the medical school and arrange for burial or cremation at the family's expense.

As another alternative, the medical school may arrange for the final disposition. In that case, the medical school designates a cemetery or crematory where the body will either be buried or cremated. The family may have the option to choose which of those methods they prefer. When the research is completed, the medical school will notify the family and make them aware that the final disposition, as directed, has taken place. If the body is buried, it may be possible for the family to be provided with the location of the grave in the designated cemetery.

If the family chooses to arrange for the burial or cremation at their own expense, an important consideration is that the family may essentially experience the loss and accompanying emotions all over again. Some people prefer this approach, and are willing to accept the emotions that may result. For others, however, the thought of making the arrangements a year or more after the death is too overwhelming, and they prefer that the medical school arrange for the final disposition.

CHAPTER SIX

UNDERSTANDING FUNERAL COSTS

When you have chosen a funeral home and set a time for an appointment, I think it's a good idea for you to prepare for the meeting by knowing about funeral costs.

When I was meeting with families, it was often helpful for them if I described the expenses as being divided into three different categories: professional services; merchandise; and cash advances.

Professional Services of the Funeral Home

Professional services of the funeral home include the arrangements conference with the family; embalming; use of the facilities and staff for the ceremony and/or visitation; and the hearse or other motor vehicles.

Perhaps the most important, for the purposes of this section, are the fees for the "Basic Services of the Funeral Director and Staff," (to which some funeral homes may add the words "and overhead"). This item represents the fee the funeral home charges for virtually any type of funeral arrangements it provides, whether it's a simple cremation with no ceremony, or something more involved and elaborate involving a casket, embalming, visitation, or other services.

This fee typically includes meeting with the family to determine the arrangements, and the "sheltering of the remains," or custody of the body, from the time of death until the time of the final disposition. Other services in this category are, obtaining burial or cremation permits, and coordination with the cemetery or crematory. The fee also includes a proportionate share of the operating expenses, or "overhead," of the funeral home, as allocated among the number of arrangements they handle each year.

Merchandise

Caskets

Before getting into the subject of caskets, I think this is a good time to talk about caskets vs. coffins. In the movies or on TV, we often see and/or hear references to a "coffin." Let's be clear that few people in the U.S. are buried in coffins these days, but the media seem intent on using that archaic term, either because they don't know the difference or in an effort to evoke dramatic imagery.

The difference between a coffin and a casket is easy to describe. The former is wider at the shoulders of the deceased and narrower at the head and foot end of the coffin. Caskets, on the other hand, are rectangular.

Casket prices are determined primarily by the material from which they are constructed, and can represent the single largest portion of the total cost of the funeral arrangements. Simply stated, caskets are divided into two categories; wood and metal. If you choose cremation, you are usually limited to selecting a casket made of wood or particleboard. Wooden caskets can be made of particleboard covered with a veneer, or hardwoods such as pine, oak, cherry, mahogany, etc. Orthodox wood caskets are available for those of the Jewish faith, and are constructed in accordance with Orthodox Jewish standards.

Metal caskets can be fabricated from steel, stainless steel, copper, or bronze. Within the category of steel casket, the price of the casket is determined primarily by the thickness of the steel, expressed as its "gauge;" a higher gauge number indicates thinner steel. The steel used in caskets is either 20-gauge or 18-gauge.

As you might expect, copper and bronze caskets are usually more expensive than those made of steel. Their thickness is expressed in terms of ounces. Copper caskets are usually constructed of 32-oz. copper, and bronze caskets may be either 32-oz. or 48-oz.

Metal caskets are also classified by the manufacturer as "protective" or "non-protective." You may also hear the terms "gasketed" or "sealed," which refer to the same principle. A protective casket can be identified by the presence of a rubber gasket attached to the top of the base of the casket. There is also some form of locking device, activated by a handle inserted into a screw-type mechanism within the casket itself. As the handle is turned, the mechanism pulls down on locking tabs on the lid of the casket to hold the two sections tightly against the gasket. This system is designed by the casket manufacturers to prevent the entrance of any air, water, or other substances into the casket itself.

There are two important points to consider about protective caskets. First, they will not permanently prevent the entrance of anything into the casket itself. As we discussed in the section about burial vaults, the casket manufacturers will also provide a warranty to the purchaser as their way of assuring the protective capabilities of this casket are indeed what the manufacturer claims them to be. As with burial vaults, the only way anyone will know whether or not that casket is performing as advertised is in the event of a disinterment. The casket itself may be disinterred, and if it's found at that time that the protective mechanism has failed, and it's within the terms of the warranty, the manufacturer will usually provide a replacement casket if the family so desires.

The second thing to know about these protective caskets is they don't in any way inhibit—and some claim they actually accelerate—the decomposition process. So while people may think the combination of embalming, a protective casket, and a protective vault will preserve the remains forever, that is simply not the case. The Federal Trade Commission could certainly prosecute a funeral director who makes any claims that these items will provide permanent preservation.

It's important to note if you choose to purchase a metal casket, there is no requirement that it have any of these protective capabilities. However, you will usually find that 18-gauge steel, copper, or bronze caskets will include this option.

Wooden caskets rarely, if ever, are advertised as protective, because by its nature wood is not impervious to the entrance of water, and wooden caskets may deteriorate more quickly than those made of metal.

The value of protective components is open to debate, and is a personal decision. To some people, these qualities I've described are very important and provide them with some comfort. Others have just scoffed at the whole notion of protective caskets and are suspicious of casket manufacturers' attempt to provide some type of warranty when it's doubtful that anyone will ever know whether the casket has functioned as advertised.

It may be necessary to arrange for "oversized" caskets to be used for people who are uncommonly tall or heavy. A funeral home will usually have one or two oversized caskets in stock, or can obtain one in a day or two from the casket distributor. When making funeral arrangements, either in advance or at the time of death, you should make the funeral director aware, as soon as possible, if you think an oversized casket might be needed.

When families are faced with selecting a casket from a funeral home, it can be a very unsettling experience. I can clearly remember feeling overwhelmed when I first walked into a casket "selection room" more than 35 years ago. It's something a lot of people aren't prepared for, and I have known people who simply refused to enter the room where the caskets were displayed. In the course of my meetings with families, I would talk with them about entering that room for the first time, describing what they would see and the differences between the caskets displayed there. I would also say candidly that there was little I could do to adequately prepare them for the experience, particularly if they had not been in the situation before.

Because many people have expressed such discomfort about being surrounded by caskets, the casket manufacturers developed an innovative system of presenting their products to consumers. Essentially, they borrowed concepts from traditional retail displays. Rather than displaying the full-sized caskets in these rooms, they use what they call "quarter cuts," which are essentially one corner of a casket, mounted on a specially designed wall. This model is representative of a full-sized casket, so families can see the wood or the metal. They can feel it, and see what the interior of that casket looks like without being overwhelmed by walking into a room of full-sized caskets. The system has proven to be quite successful. According to some funeral directors and casket manufacturers, many consumers have voiced their opinions about it being a much less intimidating environment.

Some casket manufacturers have also developed software programs they make available to funeral homes, often for a price. The programs allow families to complete the process of making funeral arrangements by choosing from options displayed on a large screen TV or monitor. In some cases, the program on the computer is connected via the Internet to the local casket distribution warehouse, so families can see a much larger selection of caskets that may interest them.

You may not be aware that renting a casket can be an alternative to buying one. Although that might sound a bit strange, it's an option for those choosing cremation that is preceded by a period of visitation and/or a funeral ceremony with the body present. In these instances, the funeral home will place the body in a temporary container that would be used for cremation, but the shell of a traditional casket would surround that temporary container. At the conclusion of the visitation or funeral service, the interior container that holds the body is simply removed from the shell and transported to the cemetery or crematory. The shell is then reused for the next family desiring similar arrangements.

There may still be some funeral homes that actually reuse an entire casket rather than renting only the shell. That's something you may want to inquire about if you are considering this option. There can be some inherent problems in reusing a casket, and some states prohibit the practice.

Historically, people bought caskets exclusively from funeral homes, but in recent years we've seen the emergence of casket stores, which can be actual storefront facilities or Internet-based, that sell caskets directly to consumers. In most states, there are no regulations prohibiting anyone from selling caskets, but some have mandated that only licensed funeral directors and/or funeral homes can legally sell them.

Such was the case in the state of Louisiana, for example. For 120 years, monks in St. Joseph Abbey, a Benedictine monastery, had been making simple pine caskets for the burial of their brothers. The public became aware of these caskets, and wanted to purchase them from the monastery. Under Louisiana law, however, only licensed funeral directors could legally sell funeral related merchandise, and funeral directors there wanted the law to be enforced to prevent the monks from selling their caskets.

The abbey enlisted the help of the Institute for Justice, and together they filed a lawsuit challenging the constitutionality of the law. Eventually, the 5th U.S. Circuit Court of Appeals struck down the law, and it appeared that the monastery could proceed with its plans to sell its caskets and use the proceeds for charitable purposes.

At the time of this writing, the Louisiana State Board of Embalmers and Funeral Directors has asked the U.S. Supreme Court to overturn the ruling of the 5th Circuit. Constitutional law is certainly beyond my expertise, but it's my opinion that regulations restricting the sale of caskets or other funeral related merchandise are unjustifiable attempts by the funeral industry to restrict competition, and will only serve to further distort and harm the reputations of the majority of funeral directors, who are committed to honorable, ethical, and legitimate service to their communities.

Returning to the topic of alternative sources of caskets, you can find caskets available online that are less expensive than those offered by funeral homes. If you choose, you can order the casket online and make arrangements to have it delivered directly to the funeral home. You need to ensure, however, that the casket seller, whether it's an actual storefront casket store or an Internet-only business, will deliver the casket as required in time for the funeral home to make the necessary preparations for the visitation or funeral ceremony.

It's a requirement of the FTC Funeral Rule that funeral homes must accept "third-party" caskets from the casket stores or other providers. The Rule also prohibits funeral homes from charging the purchaser a handling fee for accepting the delivery and working with that casket. The funeral home cannot refuse to accept the casket during the same normal delivery hours during which it would accept deliveries from their regular casket suppliers. And the funeral home cannot require a member of the family or other representative to be present at the funeral home when the casket is delivered. The funeral director is permitted, however, to suggest that a representative of the family be present to ensure that the casket delivered is the style and color that they ordered.

Outer Burial Containers

As discussed previously in this guide, cemeteries usually require, in instances of traditional earth burial, that the casket be placed in an Outer Burial Enclosure, also known as a grave liner or burial vault.

These items are usually purchased from the funeral home, and can be chosen through the use of display models illustrating the differences among those offered. Very few funeral homes have full sized outer burial containers on display due to their size and weight.

The funeral home will order the chosen grave liner or vault from the cemetery or vault company, who will install the base of the enclosure in the grave prior to the burial. After the casket is lowered into the enclosure, the cemetery or vault company personnel will put the cover in place.

Other Merchandise

Other items of funeral-related merchandise can be purchased from the funeral home. A guest register is a book that attendees at the visitation or ceremony sign. There are a wide variety of registers from which to choose, from simple spiral-bound books with paper or plastic covers, to more expensive and ornate leather-bound varieties. Other items include acknowledgement cards the family can send to people who have attended the ceremony, or sent flowers or a memorial donation. Some funeral homes maintain a flower shop on the premises or near the funeral home. Others may have relationships with one or more florists in the community and may recommend to people they use them for the purchase of their floral arrangements.

Cremation urns are available for purchase from funeral homes, as are lockets or other forms of jewelry designed to contain a small portion of the deceased's cremated remains.

Cemetery monuments, also called headstones or grave markers, can be purchased directly from funeral homes or monument companies. Many funeral homes sell monuments, though in a few states, funeral homes may be prohibited from owning a monument company. As in the case of the Louisiana regulations regarding casket sales, these regulations are increasingly seen as archaic, and I expect that many of them will be overturned in the future.

Cash Advances

Cash advances is the term used to describe the money the funeral home will distribute to others involved in the funeral arrangements, as necessary. Examples of cash advances include the cost of preparing the grave at the cemetery or the fee for the cremation process; newspaper notices; and money paid to the clergy or other person officiating at the ceremony.

Also in the cash advances category are certified copies of the death certificate, which are necessary for the purpose of probating a will, or any time proof of death is required, such as access to a joint bank account, safe deposit box, or the filing of a life insurance claim. I recommend that you obtain certified copies of the death certificate as soon as they become available. People are often surprised to learn they need many more copies than they thought they would. While it's always possible to obtain additional copies later, it may take some time, which may cause delay and inconvenience if you need to access additional accounts or encounter other situations that require a death certificate. For this reason, I recommend that you order several extra copies.

Policies regarding cash advances can vary by funeral home. Some funeral homes will assume responsibility for the distribution of these cash advances to the third parties, and the total of the cash advance items will appear on the Statement of Funeral Goods and Services Selected (SFGSS) and the final bill. For reasons related to cash-flow, other funeral homes will distribute the cash advances to the appropriate parties, but will require you to pay for them at the time the SFGSS is presented to you. Another alternative is the funeral home provides you with a detailed list of the cash advances and requires that you write checks to each of these providers, which the funeral home will then distribute.

If the funeral home is receiving any type of profit from the third party providers for handling these cash advances, the FTC Funeral Rule requires that fact to be disclosed by the funeral home on the SFGSS. The funeral home isn't required to disclose the amount of money they receive, whether it's in the form of a discount or cash payment to the funeral home for handling the transaction. But if the funeral home is receiving any form of financial benefit, the following disclaimer must appear on the SFGSS: "We charge you for our services in providing ______________," wherein the specific items subject to the discount or payment are identified, such as death notices, flowers, etc.

Package Pricing

It's not uncommon for funeral homes to present their prices in what are called "packages," a grouping of a number of items that represents the types of funeral services and merchandise that may be most frequently selected by a funeral home's customers. Depending on what arrangements the person or family wants, the packages can include the services of the funeral home and the staff, a casket or other alternative container, a burial vault if the body is to be interred in the cemetery, cremation urn, and miscellaneous items like guest registers and acknowledgement cards. Cash advances may be included, according to the funeral home's policy. Usually, one can expect there to be some savings generated by using this package approach. Funeral homes will price their packages at a moderate discount as compared to the usual itemized prices as an incentive for the purchaser to buy the package.

A funeral home will offer packages for two primary reasons: increased revenue and potentially easier decision making for the purchaser.

First, it can be beneficial to the funeral home to present their offerings this way, because it may entice purchasers to buy items that they may not otherwise buy on an itemized basis. For example, if the use of a limousine to transport the family in the funeral procession is included in a package, a family may decide that they may as well use it. However, if they were selecting individual items from the GPL, they may be inclined to omit the limousine and save some money.

Funeral homes typically require that packages be purchased on an "all or nothing" basis, meaning that the package is available only as presented. If the purchaser wants to omit a particular item included in the package, (such as the limousine, in the previous example), there is no corresponding reduction in the package price. In that case, the buyer would either pay the package price and decline to use the limo, or abandon the package and choose individual items from the GPL.

In regard to the second reason for package pricing, it has been reported by funeral home owners that a substantial number of families prefer to buy packaged funeral arrangements, rather than on an item-by-item basis from the GPL, because it eases the burden of decision making. The preference may be the result of a desire to save money, minimize the number of decisions to be made, "do what most people do," or a need to just finish the arrangements discussion as quickly as possible.

Package pricing does not, however, relieve the funeral home from the obligation to provide purchasers with the GPL. The FTC mandates that a "package price list" can be distributed together with, but not in place of, the itemized GPL.

Funeral Home Profits

In my experience, most people think that funeral homes make an enormous profit on every funeral they provide. I assume that one of the reasons they think this is because the funeral industry has received quite a lot of bad press over the years, beginning with the book by Jessica Mitford and continuing to current news stories about funeral costs.

Appearances also contribute to this impression. Funeral homes often maintain large and well-decorated buildings, well-dressed employees, and expensive hearses and other vehicles. In reality, however, the average funeral home's profit margin is quite small, given the investment the owners have in their facilities, vehicles, and staffing, to say nothing of the emotion, commitment, and stress their business entails.

Staffing represents the single largest operating expense of the average funeral home. No funeral home owner or manager can predict when their services will be needed, and it's virtually impossible for a funeral home to routinely maintain the staffing levels required for their busiest times. Yet funeral home employees must be ready twenty-four hours a day, 365 days a year, to respond when contacted by families. On average, salary and benefits costs account for about 30% to 40% of a funeral home's total revenue. And to be clear, funeral directors are typically not paid exorbitant salaries. For the year 2012, the U.S. Bureau of Labor Statistics reported the median annual salary for morticians, undertakers, and funeral directors (all the same jobs) at $52, 390.

During my years with the association, one of the services we provided to the members was a survey and analysis of their individual revenue, expenses, and profitability, as compared to the averages and medians for all the members participating in the survey. If a funeral home achieved 9% profit before tax, it was considered by our standards to be well managed. For a variety of reasons, not the least of which is the increased cremation rate and the trend toward more people choosing memorial services as opposed to traditional funeral services, funeral homes have seen their profitability rates decline significantly. According to published reports, profitability of about 6% of total revenue is now the average.

For purposes of illustration, consider that the National Funeral Directors Association (nfda.org) reports that in 2012, the average cost of an adult funeral was $8,343, including the services of the funeral home, the casket, and outer burial enclosure (the total does not include cemetery expenses, monument costs or cash advances). Accordingly, the average funeral home's profit is roughly $500 per funeral, which I suspect is far below what most people would estimate.

It's not my intention to act as an advocate for the funeral industry. I offer this information factually and objectively, in the hope that it will provide insight into the somewhat mysterious nature of the profession, and will help to dispel some of the misinformation and undeserved criticism the industry has endured for so many years. If fact, I have never understood why funeral home owners and managers aren't eager to talk about the money they make (or don't make), because in reality, it's usually far less than most people imagine.

Within the context of funeral home profits, I think it's important to consider the more intangible aspects of a funeral director's life. When you hear the phrase funeral director, or undertaker, or mortician, a caricature probably comes to mind. The cadaverously thin and pale man, dressed in black, wringing his hands with seemingly fake sympathy, while mentally counting the coins he'll draw from your pockets for his services. This portrayal of funeral directors has been popular in the media, and society in general, since the funeral business first began (and to be truthful, I have known one or two funeral directors who have contributed to this perception), and I have little hope that it will change anytime soon.

In reality, most who choose a career in the funeral industry have nothing at all in common with the stereotype. They do not seek great financial reward, and many view the job as a calling. They are caring, dedicated men and women who are motivated each day by the satisfaction they receive from helping people during a time of tremendous loss and personal tragedy. Few outside the business can appreciate the effect that a note or other expression of gratitude from a family can have on a funeral director. I have on occasion been made to feel almost like a member of the family I was working with. Although I sometimes heard more about family issues and personalities than I wanted or expected, I regarded and still remember those occasions as a privilege.

There are also the challenging aspects of the job. Funeral directors are often the recipients of survivors' misdirected anger at the death of their parent, child, sibling, or other relative. When funeral directors make their occupations known to others, at parties or other social events, they may endure tired jokes, innumerable anecdotes, and undeserved suspicion and distrust from people who have never experienced a funeral director's compassion and commitment. They work long hours, witness unspeakably horrific events, and are continually surrounded by people in extreme emotional distress.

Funeral home owners and their employees, especially those in small funeral homes with only two or three staff members, routinely sacrifice time that could be spent with their families during holidays, at their kids' baseball games or other school activities, birthday parties, and other events many of us take for granted.

It's not uncommon for this stress to take its toll, because they're human too. I have never known a good funeral director to become insensitive to the plight of the families that he or she serves. If some do, they should find another occupation, because their callousness probably prevents them from working effectively with families. Unquestionably, they must maintain a professional balance between empathy and effectiveness, and I know that many funeral directors, embalmers, and their support staff will hug their spouses, children, partners, or others just a bit more tightly at the end of a particularly difficult day. Please try to keep this in mind when meeting and working with professionals in the funeral industry.

Paying for a Funeral

In the early years of my career, most funeral homes didn't maintain strict payment policies. Instead, the funeral home would send a bill to the family sometime after the funeral, and hope for payment within thirty days or so. Many funeral homes still continue this practice.

However, as a result of decreasing profits and tighter cash flows, funeral homes are adopting more stringent payment policies than had been typical in the past. It's not uncommon now for them to require families to pay, when the arrangements have been finalized or prior to the ceremony or final disposition, either (a) the total amount of the cash advances; or (b) the total amount due for all services, merchandise, and cash advances.

Funeral homes typically accept payment in the form of cash, check, or credit card. I don't know of any funeral homes that accept or sell gift certificates. If the deceased had a life insurance policy, it may be possible to assign the proceeds of the policy to the funeral home, but only after the funeral director has verified the total amount of the death benefit that is available, which may have been reduced from the original face amount by loans or other factors.

I think a case can be made that this is a reasonable evolution in funeral homes' business practices. I believe it's generally acknowledged that it's not possible for someone to purchase anything in his or her community for $500, or $1,000, or $8,000, or whatever the amount may be, and not make payment in full at the time of purchase or guarantee payment of the total amount before the merchandise or service is delivered. In my view, the purchase of funeral services should not be treated any differently.

Although it may not be apparent, purchasers may also benefit from these more stringent payment policies. Sometimes, people spend more money at a funeral home than they can afford, especially if they are not faced with an immediate requirement to pay for what they buy. It can be argued that grief, guilt, and confusion play a significant role in this behavior, and people may subconsciously tell themselves that they will figure out how to pay for these things "when the time comes."

No funeral home owner is anxious to be faced with uncollectible accounts receivable. When people spend more than they can afford at a funeral home, the outcome is not good for anyone involved. The family is now faced with a financial obligation they are unable to meet, and they may feel resentment toward the funeral home for having sold them things they didn't need. The funeral home will not be paid for the services it has provided. Any effort to collect on these accounts through the use of collection agencies or legal means can be damaging to the funeral home's reputation in the community, as those with no knowledge of the circumstances see the funeral home owner as greedy and uncaring.

If this scenario is repeated very often, the funeral home will be forced to increase its charges to the people that can afford to pay, in much the same way as hospitals need to adjust their emergency room charges to recover the cost of caring for patients that are uninsured and cannot pay for the services they receive.

To avoid creating a financial obligation that you don't want or can't afford, you should clearly understand the funeral home's payment policy before finalizing any purchase decisions.

Financial Assistance

If you don't have sufficient resources to pay for a funeral, I strongly suggest that you make that clear to the funeral director at the beginning of your discussion.

Often, funeral homes will make special arrangements to accommodate people with limited resources, and I have never known a funeral home that turned away someone that needed their services but couldn't afford to pay for them.

In addition, there may be benefits, either through Medicaid or other public assistance programs, which the funeral director can advise you about. There are also national cemeteries and state-run military cemeteries in which veterans may be buried without charge, and for whom cemetery monuments and burial allowances may be available.

Prepayment

Once you have decided upon the type of arrangements you would like, either for yourself or someone else, you may choose to pay for them in advance, potentially sparing your survivors the responsibility for payment for the funeral services or other arrangements you have directed. It's important, however, for you to know about the benefits and potential risks inherent in pre-paying for a funeral.

When you have made all the necessary decisions, the funeral home will present the Statement of Funeral Goods and Services Selected, which includes a description of the items you have chosen and the related prices. Review this document carefully to ensure that it includes only those items you have selected, sign it, and retain a copy.

Several payment methods may be presented to you. You may pay the entire amount in one payment to the funeral home, by cash, check, or credit card. You may choose to purchase an insurance policy, for which the funeral home is the beneficiary. The insurance policy can usually be paid either in a single premium or in multiple premiums over a period of time. Some states prohibit insurance policies for the prepayment of funeral expenses, and require any prepaid monies be deposited in a trust. Other states prohibit trusts in favor of insurance, so as you can see, it's important for you to clearly understand what options are available to you.

In the past there have been a number of cases where the people responsible for administering the trust were found to have engaged in very risky investment vehicles or strategies, which have resulted in the loss of millions of dollars. There have also been instances where people have fled with the money, leaving the funeral homes and their customers with no access to the funds.

My general philosophy and advice is that you must consider this decision with the same care and diligence with which you would approach any significant financial transaction. Prepayment of a funeral can involve several thousand dollars, and it's critically important for you to understand where your money is, how safe it's, and how it's going to be invested.

If preneed insurance is available, there are some important questions to ask of the funeral home. What is the A.M. Best rating of the insurance company? How long has it been in existence, and where can you obtain more information about its history? Is the face amount of the policy, i.e., the amount to be paid upon death, guaranteed, and if so, for how long? If you decide to use a different funeral home, how can you change the beneficiary named in the policy? What happens to the policy if the insurance company goes out of business?

If you are going to be depositing your money in a trust, there are different questions to ask. How is the trust administered, where will your money be deposited, and how will it be invested? Does the Federal Deposit Insurance Corporation (FDIC), insure the money, as it does your checking account? What types of investments does the trust manager prefer?

Regardless of the payment method, there are other important considerations. What about cancellation? If you give your money to the funeral home to pay for a funeral service in advance, and you change your mind in the future, what is the funeral home's cancellation policy? This is important, because in some states, funeral homes may be required to invest only a percentage of the total money they receive. So, for example, you may pay $8,000 to a funeral home, but the funeral home may be required to deposit only 90% of that amount into the trust, and permitted to retain the remaining 10% as an administrative fee. So if you want to cancel that prepayment at some point in the future, will you be receiving 100% of your investment?

Another essential issue is portability. If you move from one state to another, or if you want to move your prepaid funeral arrangements from Funeral Home A to Funeral Home B in the same community, how easy is it to do that? Is it merely a matter of signing over the amount of money from Funeral Home A to Funeral Home B? Do you need to withdraw the money to make that transfer on your own?

One of the most important distinctions of prepaid funeral contracts is whether the agreement is revocable or irrevocable. In the case of revocable agreements, the purchaser has the option of cancelling the agreement and receiving all or part of the principle and interest in the account.

Irrevocable agreements cannot be cancelled, the money paid into the account cannot be refunded, and it cannot be used for any purpose other than being applied toward the payment of the funeral expenses. When people are applying to receive Medicaid benefits, they may set money aside in an irrevocable agreement for funeral expenses, and those funds wouldn't be considered as assets when determining their eligibility. A funeral director or financial planner can advise you on the requirements that exist in the state in which the Medicaid recipient lives.

When the concept of preneed payment first emerged years ago, many funeral homes guaranteed the prices quoted in the agreement as soon as the total amount was paid in full. In this case, no additional money was required when the death occurred, regardless of how many years elapsed, as long as the arrangements remained essentially the same as specified in the contract.

The funeral home could justify the price guarantee because the money was being invested, either in a savings account, insurance policy, or trust, and the funeral home was the beneficiary. The principal and interest or other investment income that accrued on the account would be paid to the funeral home and, it was presumed, would cover any increase in their costs over the years. Similarly, increases in the death benefit of an insurance policy over a period of time would provide the funeral home with the proceeds necessary to offset inflation. In a high-interest economy, it's possible that the growth of the trust or insurance policy will be sufficient to prevent any shortfall of funds when the person dies.

We have already explored the decreasing profitability levels of funeral homes. That, in part, has led to a change in the philosophy of many funeral homes, and some will no longer guarantee the charges specified in the preneed contract. They will take the position that the then current charges will apply when the death occurs, and the funds available in the preneed account or insurance policy will be applied toward payment of the charges. The family will be responsible for making up any shortfall that exists, whether as a result of poor investment performance, price increases for the funeral home's services, or a combination of factors.

It's understandable to me why funeral homes would be reluctant to guarantee any prices in the future, particularly in the low-interest economy we've experienced over the past several years. It's possible that the growth of the investment or insurance policy has not kept pace with increases in the funeral homes' operating expenses, or casket and outer burial container costs. Another risk factor for them is that they have no way to control what cemeteries, newspapers, or other third party suppliers charge for their services. Even if funeral homes still guarantee the prices specified in the prepayment agreement, it's not unusual to find that cash advances are excluded from that guarantee.

Conversely, let's say a funeral home has been particularly successful at investing the money it has received as prepayment. When the death occurs, there is more money in the account than is required to pay for the funeral arrangements at the current prices. As you consider a prepaid funeral agreement, it's important for you to ask what happens to the money that is left in the account. If there is excess, it's the position of some funeral homes that because they have borne the risk of the performance of that investment, they also deserve the reward for having assumed the risk for that period of time. Other funeral homes willingly return any excess funds, when permitted, to the next of kin or person responsible for the funeral arrangements. In some areas, it's required that excess funds in the account be returned to the survivors when the services have been provided.

Generally, and especially in those circumstances where the funeral home's prices are not guaranteed, you should think seriously about whether a prepaid funeral agreement is in your best interest. Some people will say they trust the funeral home, they've known the funeral home owner for many years, and they think it's a worthwhile investment, offering them peace of mind. They don't want to place any financial or decision-making burden on survivors, and they are willing to assume the financial risk, even if the prices aren't guaranteed.

You may want to consider other options, which may be as simple as determining what the present cost of the arrangements will be, and either setting aside a lump sum or periodic "installments" in an investment vehicle you control. These funds can be deposited in a joint account with your next of kin or other designated person who will be responsible for the funeral arrangements and would therefore have access to that money in order to pay the funeral home.

If the funeral home doesn't guarantee the prices established in the preneed contract, then I would argue there is very little benefit, beyond peace of mind, to paying the funeral home in advance. That's not meant to cast any doubts on the integrity of a funeral home owner in any given community, but is based on the combination of a lack of real financial benefit and the potential for mismanagement of the prepaid funds. Often, the funeral home owners who deposit preneed funds into the master trusts available to them have no direct control over the investment philosophy or performance. They are reliant on the people that have been chosen to manage the trust, and funeral homes are put in very difficult situations when it's discovered that the performance of a trust has been less than anticipated or, even worse, money has been spent or mismanaged in violation of the trust's requirements.

In recent years, some preneed trusts have been administered by state funeral home associations, who retain the services of a financial adviser and/or institution to manage the trusts' investments. In its role as the trust administrator, an association generates revenue for itself, which is not necessarily wrong, but does present some potential problems.

In the state of Wisconsin, it was recently reported that there was a shortfall of at least $21 million in the Wisconsin Funeral Trust, a preneed "Master Trust" that had been established by the Wisconsin Funeral Directors Association, affecting more than 10,000 people who had money on deposit. The Wisconsin Department of Justice and Wisconsin Department of Financial Institutions have alleged that, among other charges, the trust's investments were too risky and in violation of Wisconsin law. As a result, the Dane County Circuit Court appointed a receiver to preserve the trust's remaining assets and attempt to recover the shortfall from the responsible parties.

The Court also approved a settlement agreement between the Wisconsin Funeral Trust and the funeral homes that had deposited money in it. Funeral homes choosing to participate in the settlement promise that consumers will receive the goods and services as described in the preneed agreements, and the funeral homes will be immune from further legal action.

Funeral homes in these circumstances are faced with potentially significant economic losses, because they may be recovering only a small percentage of the money that they, under normal circumstances, would have received from the trust when they provide the services. In addition, they may have suffered bad publicity when the shortfall was made public. In the minds of some people, the situation may also cast doubt on the judgment of the funeral home owner and may indeed damage the reputation of the funeral home in the community, which the funeral home owners have probably worked very hard to develop and maintain over a period of many years.

While I don't mean to suggest that the Wisconsin Funeral Trust debacle should be seen as a representation of all preneed trusts, I offer it as an example of what can happen and why it's important for you to consider your prepayment options carefully.

Chapter Seven

Making it Meaningful

All of the elements of funeral planning that I've discussed so far in this guide have been related to the basic, practical decisions you'll need to make. But planning a funeral or other tribute also involves additional, creative aspects that can help you to create a personalized, meaningful tribute that accomplishes three things:

1. It honors the unique life of the person who has died, reflecting his or her unique personality, career, and interests.
2. It meets the survivors' emotional, spiritual, cultural, and economic needs.
3. It helps the survivors with the transition to life without the person they've loved, and to begin the emotional healing process.

Planning in advance makes it easier to design a tribute that meets these criteria without the sadness, confusion, and feelings of being overwhelmed that typically follow the death of someone we care about. It also allows decisions to be made without the perceived time pressure many people feel after a death has occurred.

During my years as a practicing funeral director, I estimate I participated in or observed more than two thousand funerals, and fewer than 10 percent of them involved any type of personalization. In many cases the only part of one funeral that was different from all the others was the information that appeared in the obituary. I recall sitting in churches and other places of worship where I heard the same ritual that had been conducted for any number of people over the preceding weeks or months.

It is not my intention to diminish the importance of established religious ceremonies; I know that many people take immeasurable comfort in the rites and traditions that are integral parts of their spiritual beliefs. But I also believe that people should have the option and opportunity to create personalized, meaningful tributes that honor the unique life of the person that has died. Traditional ceremonies and personalized tributes needn't be mutually exclusive, and combining them as desired can produce comforting, inspiring, and gratifying experiences.

Today, the baby boomer generation places a lot of emphasis on the customization of many things, from weddings, vacations, and automobiles, to the technological equipment we use. Those preferences for personalization are being reflected in the types of memorial services or funerals we create. We are used to having things our way, and the trend toward creating unique end-of-life events is certainly a natural extension of our desires for personalization.

When you hear the term personalization, you probably think it's a bit abstract in the context of funeral planning. I suggest that it's simply the process of incorporating personal, meaningful elements into a funeral or memorial ceremony, (or tribute, or whatever you would prefer to call it), in a way that recognizes and honors the unique personality and attributes of the person who has died, and helps us to say goodbye.

Personalization certainly doesn't need to be complicated, burdensome, or expensive. It can be something as simple as arranging photographs of the person around the room where the visitation and ceremony will take place. Many funeral homes now have the ability to create videos assembled from photographs provided to them by the family. The videos will be playing on large TVs or monitors around the funeral home or other venue where the ceremony will be held, and help people to remember particular characteristics and events in the life of the deceased and the qualities of that person that affected their own lives.

It's not uncommon to display items that reflect the deceased's personality, occupation, and interests. I've seen people place items such as fishing poles, baseball memorabilia, or even a motorcycle near the casket or somewhere in the room. If a particular item represents a special interest of the person that has died, it can be the catalyst for personal stories that can evoke both sorrow and joy, which can be very helpful in beginning the emotional healing process.

Of course, there are no limits to personalization. I've known of a few examples, one of which was the funeral of a former racecar driver, whose family arranged for the funeral ceremony to be conducted at a racetrack, with the family seated in the stands. At the conclusion of the ceremony, the hearse, with the casket inside, took one final lap around the track before heading to the cemetery.

For the funeral of an elementary school teacher, the funeral home staff removed much of the furniture that would normally be in the visitation room, and replaced it with desks and chairs from the school where the lady taught, and displayed notes and drawings her students had created in her honor.

Another example I recall is the death of a baby whose parents were members of a Native American tribe. It was their custom that when an infant died, he or she was buried in a "papoose," a child carrier that is usually strapped to a parent's back, for carrying the infant during the course of their day. It was very important to them this tradition be respected and followed, and they wanted him to be buried in a papoose. The cemetery required an outer burial container, as most cemeteries do, but there was no requirement for a casket. So we arrived at a compromise that involved the baby being placed in the papoose, and the family members placing the papoose in the vault at the cemetery. It was a simple way to meet the requirements of the cemetery that also was in keeping with the very important traditions of the family and their tribe.

As I hope you can see, something that doesn't involve much expense or a lot of effort can create a very special and unique opportunity to honor someone's life.

Part of the process of selecting a funeral home or other provider, as discussed earlier, involves choosing one that has the ability and desire to be creative, to be willing to explore the various ways in which the person can be uniquely honored, and suggest to the family members ways in which that can be achieved.

Regardless of the nature of the arrangements you are making, part of what you are paying for when you engage the services of a funeral director is his or her experience, knowledge, and willingness to help create a tribute that is right for you. You should expect that guidance without having to ask for it.

I believe it's the responsibility and the obligation of the funeral director to make suggestions to you about ways in which you might honor the person you love. Unfortunately, it has been my experience that some people perceive these suggestions as an attempt on the part of the funeral director to sell them more services and increase the funeral home's profit.

While that may be true in some cases, a conscientious funeral director will offer suggestions for the purpose of helping you to create an experience that truly is unique and appropriate. It is his or her job to make you aware of your options. If they involve additional expense, you are still ultimately in control of the decisions, and have the power to accept the ideas if they are affordable, appropriate, and meaningful for you and your family. If I were helping people make funeral arrangements today, I wouldn't want any of them to come back to me weeks after the funeral and say to me, "You never told us we could do *that*!"

It's also important to include as many family members as possible in the planning of these tributes.

Different people have different ideas. Not all of them will be incorporated into the ceremony, but I believe that by virtue of these family discussions, you can enable others that are in emotional pain to feel involved in the process, which may be helpful to them as they mourn.

The way people respond to the death of a family member varies widely. I've seen instances where it was extremely divisive, and caused conflicts that had been suppressed or ignored by family members to rise to the surface. I have also seen it bring families together, when they relied upon and supported each other through the pain of their common sorrow.

It has been said that grief shared can be grief diminished. The days following the death of someone you care about present an opportunity for you and your family to share your grief, and for those outside of the family to express sympathy and understanding, regardless of the type of ceremony, where it takes place, or how many people are in attendance.

There are two examples I'll share that demonstrate the different needs and preferences of family members. The first is the funeral I arranged for a police officer who died in the line of duty. It was the first time in the city's history that a police officer had died this way, and at the funeral home there were lines of people waiting to pay their respects to the officer and offer their words of support to his family. It was estimated that more than 250 cars, many of them representing law enforcement departments from near and far, formed the procession to the cemetery. It was obvious to me that this family took immeasurable comfort in this public demonstration of honor, respect, and gratitude for the sacrifice the officer and his family had made.

I also arranged for a woman to be cremated. It was her husband's desire that a very private and brief ceremony take place when the cremated remains were buried at the cemetery. He asked me if I alone would accompany him and say a few prayers at the graveside. I recall meeting him at the cemetery on that rainy morning. As he and I stood at the grave, I recited a few prayers and he silently cried. There was no outpouring of sentiment or support from the community, but that was the tribute he felt most appropriate; what he perhaps needed to do.

Funeral Celebrants

It has been reported that an increasing number of people in North America do not belong to churches or other places of worship, or adhere to any of the mainstream religions. In some instances, they may be at a loss to determine who will officiate at either the funeral or the memorial service for the person who has died. In response, there has been an emergence of "funeral celebrants" who conduct services that may incorporate a religious component, but also seek to create a tribute that may be more meaningful for families and reflect the unique characteristics, career, and interests of the deceased.

If this option is of interest to you, ask the funeral director or others in your community about their experiences with funeral celebrants. Many funeral homes have celebrants on their staffs, or have experience with individuals in the community who provide this service. To my knowledge, there are no generally accepted qualifications. There are companies and professionals that specialize in the training of funeral celebrants, but while that is indicative of someone having taken a more formal approach to developing their skills, there may be others available to you that are equally talented and capable of creating a personalized and meaningful tribute.

I would like to offer a few words about the influence of others on your decisions. When a death occurs, you may receive a lot of well-intentioned advice from friends, relatives, neighbors, and others, each with a story about their own personal experiences, good or bad, or their own opinions on the "right" way to plan a funeral.

Some of this advice may be an attempt to encourage you to use, or avoid, a particular funeral home or other provider. Other comments may be intended to help you save money, by choosing simple arrangements over more costly and unnecessary alternatives. And still others may try to influence you to buy services and other items that you really don't want.

I am not suggesting that these words of advice are insincere, or motivated by anything other than an authentic desire to help you through a very difficult time. Nor do I recommend that you dismiss them. My point is that the decisions you make must be those that are best for you in every sense. It's possible to listen to advice without following it. It's my hope that this guide has encouraged you to think about planning a tribute, helped you to talk with your family about it, and empowered you to face the subject with confidence and clarity.

I will close with a story about Gloria, a great friend of mine whose husband, Vern, died of leukemia in his mid-80s. They had been married for 14 years, and it was impossible to be in their presence and not see how happy they were together.

When Vern and Gloria learned that his illness was incurable, they began to plan his memorial service. Vern had been a radio and television sound engineer for most of his career, and he was widely recognized as exceptionally talented, a consummate professional. Vern's love of his career extended well beyond his employment; he had built his own recording studio in the basement of their home, and had been known to lovingly restore old recording equipment, including a control board that he graciously donated to a local radio station.

The career that Vern loved was the focal point of the memorial service he and Gloria created. Vern selected music that held special meaning for them from their first date on. The selections he chose, mostly from the 1950s, '60s, and '70s, contained words that expressed his love for Gloria and hers for him. The ceremony represented the seasons of the year, which also paralleled the seasons of their lives together.

They asked a close friend, who is a popular radio personality, to serve as the master of ceremonies. They made a list of people to be invited to share their memories during the service, and entrusted to Vern's colleagues the details of obtaining the proper equipment and its placement in the church where the service would take place.

As I was seated in the church, I could see a sound engineer seated at a control board, controlling the microphones and an audio system with very high quality speakers, through which the chosen music was playing.

The memorial programs distributed to those in attendance included the following greeting, written by Vern as he grew weaker just a few days before he died, and later discovered by Gloria:

> *"Good afternoon, folks. I wish to thank you for gathering here this day in the company of many of Gloria's and my very special friends and family members. We are not here to grieve, but to celebrate the wonderful association and good times we have shared with you. As you listen to this music, know that each song has special meaning for us."*

The ceremony was divided into several segments, each of which included a musical selection and remembrances shared by one of the invited speakers. The widely known and respected master of ceremonies welcomed everyone and shared a few words about his long friendship with Vern. Next to speak was Vern's son, followed by colleagues with whom Vern had worked for many years. They spoke about his value to them as a mentor and his reputation as a perfectionist. They shared stories of Vern's many words of encouragement, sense of humor, and acts of kindness. Some recalled tearfully that they could always rely on Vern. Whenever there was a technical problem or emergency, Vern would be the one who would sort it out and make everything all right again.

The ceremony concluded with the words of one of Gloria's friends, now a chaplain intern, who had spoken at their wedding. She had since become a close friend of both of them and visited Vern frequently during his illness, providing comfort to him simply by her presence.

The entire memorial service was recorded (as one would expect for a sound engineer), and a few weeks afterward, Gloria presented to a few of us CDs containing the audio portion of the ceremony. People were so moved by the way the ceremony was designed and conducted, and by the way it honored Vern, that for weeks, Gloria received requests from friends for a copy of the CD.

I spoke with her a couple of days after the ceremony and asked how she was doing. She said, "Well, that night after the service, as I got into bed, I was thinking about the day and how nice Vern's ceremony was, and I said to myself, 'There. We did it. It was perfect for him, and I feel at peace."

That is the ultimate goal. To reflect on the final tribute each of us creates for the people we love and to be able to say that it was perfect. That it captured the essence of the person who has meant so much to us. And while I'm not suggesting that any of this will remove the pain, loss, sadness, and grief, I do believe it can be a source of comfort as we begin to face life without the one we have loved. I hope you will find inspiration in the story of Gloria and Vern; that it will take away some of the fear and discomfort you have about planning a funeral and illustrate the many possibilities available to you. I also hope it will encourage you to begin a discussion with your family to create a meaningful and appropriate tribute, in the knowledge that planning ahead for life's inescapable event can ultimately reduce stress and confusion for you or those you care about.

EMERGENCY GUIDELINES

FIRST STEPS TO TAKE WHEN A DEATH OCCURS

This is the condensed version of the information you need if you are suddenly faced with the responsibility for making funeral arrangements for someone you care about. Emotions, fears, and lack of experience in funeral planning all combine to produce confusion, apprehension, and feelings of vulnerability. If the death was unexpected, the overwhelming sense of loss and a perceived urgency to complete the funeral arrangements may be intensified, and decision-making becomes more difficult.

Equipped with the following guidelines, however, you can be in control of the process, prioritize your decision-making, reduce the accompanying chaos, and arrive at decisions that meet your spiritual, cultural, emotional, and economic needs and preferences. This section will examine each of these items:

1. Know Your Rights
2. Choose and Contact a Funeral Home or Other Provider
3. Gather Required Information
4. Take Your Time
5. Consider Your Options
6. Make It Meaningful

Know Your Rights

The first step in taking control of funeral arrangements is knowing your rights. In the US, the Federal Trade Commission regulates the funeral industry through its Funeral Rule. The Rule requires a number of disclosures and actions on the part of the funeral provider, designed to make it easier for consumers to compare funeral home services and prices. For example, the Rule requires funeral homes to:

- Provide price information by telephone
- Provide a written "General Price List" (GPL) to anyone who inquires in person about funeral arrangements, as soon as the discussion begins.
- Present Casket and Outer Burial Container price lists prior to the review and/or selection of those items
- Provide the purchaser with a written "Statement of Funeral Goods and Services Selected" after the decisions are made, but prior to payment

You should expect to receive the itemized General Price List at the beginning of any discussion about funeral arrangements. Ask questions about any areas not clear to you, and postpone any decisions until you are comfortable with the information and options presented to you.

Choose and Contact a Funeral Home or Other Provider

In years past, the decision about which funeral home to call when a family member died was probably not a decision at all. For generations, one funeral home in the community had provided funerals for most, if not all members of a given family, and the loyalty that developed was strong and enduring.

While that is still true for some, the mobility of today's society has left many people without a designated "family" funeral home. People who have relocated to a different community may find themselves, suddenly faced with the unexpected death of a spouse, child, or other family member, and are completely unfamiliar with the reputations and abilities of the funeral homes in the area.

If you are among those who have experience with and/or a preference for a particular funeral home, your decision may have already been made (although reading the rest of this section may be helpful). If you haven't determined which funeral home you would call in an emergency, consider the following steps:

- Ask friends, coworkers, clergy, and other community professionals about their experiences.
- Telephone several funeral homes in your area. Ask questions and try to get a sense of the staff's attitude, knowledge, courtesy, and professionalism. You may also ask about the charges for various services the funeral home can provide.

- After completing your initial telephone research, schedule an appointment with one or more of the funeral homes that you feel could be best for you. During that appointment (which should be free of charge), you should take the opportunity to tour the facility, learn more about the options available to you, and get specific price information for the arrangements you are considering.
- Obtain and refer to the General Price Lists (discussed in Chapter 3 of this guide) to compare the services and prices of different funeral homes. While cost may not be the best or most critical factor to consider when choosing a funeral home, it's an important consideration for many people.

Gather Required Information

You will need to provide the funeral home or other provider with the following information that must be included on the death certificate:

Death Certificate Information

Name: ____
First Middle Last

Date of Birth:________________ Birthplace:________________________
Month / Day / Year City and State or Country if not in U.S.

Social Security Number: _______ - _____ - ________

Father's Full Name: ________________________________Birthplace: ______________
State

Mother's Name: ____________________________ Birthplace: ________________
First Maiden State

Informant's Name:__________________________________Relationship:______________

Informant's Mailing Address:____
No. & Street; City; State; Zip Code

Is deceased of Hispanic origin?: ❑Yes ❑No Race: ________________________
White, Black, Native American, etc.

Education (Highest Grade Completed): ___________________
Elementary / Secondary College
0-12 1-4; 5+

Marital Status: ❑Married ❑Never Married ❑Widowed ❑Divorced

Last Spouse ____
(Please include Maiden Name, if applicable):

Usual Occupation (Prior, if retired): ____________________________

Kind of Business or Industry: __________________________________

Are you a U.S. war veteran: ❑yes ❑no

If yes, please specify war: ____________________________ If you are a veteran and cannot locate your certificate of discharge from military service, you may request a copy by visiting the website of the National Archives at http://www.archives.gov/veterans/military-service-records/.

Take Your Time

When a death occurs and arrangements have not been planned in advance, you may feel pressured into making decisions quickly. If the death is unexpected, the feeling of urgency may be greater, because it's unlikely that you and/or family members have considered the responsibilities and options facing you. When these decisions are made without enough time to think them through and consider alternatives, the potential for anxiety, confusion, and regret can be increased.

In most cases, you should try to resist the urge to make decisions quickly, and take whatever time is necessary to finalize funeral arrangements that incorporate your spiritual, cultural, emotional, and economic needs. Some religious denominations require burial or cremation of the deceased within a specific period of time following the death, but in the absence of those requirements, there is generally no need for decisions about funeral arrangements to be influenced by time pressure.

If you have selected a funeral home, the funeral home personnel should be contacted, advised of the death and instructed to transfer the deceased to their facility. It may also be possible to schedule an appointment with the funeral director to discuss the arrangements.

If the person died at home, it will be necessary for his or her attending physician or other authorized person to make the legal pronouncement of death, which must be done before the body can be taken from the home. Family members will be advised when this process has been completed, and can then contact a funeral home. If you or other family members want or need to spend time with the person before the body is removed from the home, you should do so. I suggest that you notify the funeral home to advise them of the death and establish a time for them to arrive, or let them know that you will call them when the time is appropriate.

During this initial telephone conversation, the funeral director may ask you if the deceased is to be embalmed. Embalming is a process that uses preservative chemicals to temporarily postpone the inevitable decomposition of the body. Only in rare circumstances does law require embalming, and you typically have the option of choosing funeral arrangements that don't require embalming. Funeral homes usually require embalming if the arrangements include a public "viewing" of the body in an open casket. If you are undecided about public viewing, authorization for embalming can be postponed until the decision is made. If the possibility of an open casket exists, however, you may wish to give permission to the funeral home to proceed with the embalming in order to keep that option available.

Consider Your Options

When arranging a funeral or other memorial tribute, it's important to remember that you generally have a number of options available to you that can be tailored to meet your needs and preferences. For example, people usually have choices about whether to include a visitation period (or "wake"); the place where the ceremony will be held; if the deceased's body will be present for the ceremony; and the method of "final disposition" of the body, which could be earth burial, cremation, entombment, or anatomical donation.

The decision about the method of final disposition is only one of many alternatives to consider when arranging a funeral or other memorial tribute.

Many people are placing increasing importance on the personalization of the ceremony; creating a meaningful, "customized" event that reflects the unique qualities, achievements and interests of the person that has died.

Make It Meaningful

During my years as a practicing funeral director, I estimate that I participated in or observed more than 2,000 funerals. Of that number, perhaps 10% involved any type of personalization – the use of elements that truly reflected the personality, character, interests, and accomplishments of the person who had died. In many instances, the only part of any one funeral that was different from all the others was the information that appeared in the obituary.

Today people are placing much more emphasis on the "customization" of funeral and memorial ceremonies. Members of the baby boomer generation have grown accustomed to having things our way, from vacations to weddings to websites, and the trend toward unique end-of-life events is a natural extension of those desires.

Personalization doesn't need to be complicated, burdensome, or expensive. It can be as simple as arranging photographs of the deceased around the room where the visitation and/or ceremony will take place. Many funeral homes can arrange for the production of a video montage of photographs that will be played continuously during these times.

Various items that reflect the interests of the person who has died, such as fishing poles, baseball memorabilia, or a motorcycle, can be placed near the casket (if there is one) or anywhere that visitors can see. These items will often be the catalyst for personal stories that evoke both sorrow and joy, both of which can be helpful in the emotional healing process.

Of course, there are almost no limits to personalization. I have known of one family honoring a former racecar driver by having his funeral at a racetrack, with the hearse bearing his body making a lap around the track before proceeding to the cemetery. In another example, the chapel of a funeral home was adorned with small desks and drawings from students to pay tribute to a teacher.

Take time to talk with family members and close friends about ways to personalize the ceremony. Don't hesitate to ask the funeral director to relate examples of personalization that have been used in the past. Most likely, he or she will be eager to help design a ceremony that incorporates your ideas with methods you may not have considered. Depending on the amount of extra work required of the funeral home staff, these special touches may not result in any additional costs.

Please remember that funerals are for the living. Don't hesitate to do what you can to help you and your family through what many people have described as the worst time in their lives.

List of Resources

The following resources are provided strictly as an aid to your research. Their inclusion here does not constitute my endorsement or promotion.

U.S. Federal Trade Commission
www.consumer.ftc.gov/articles/0300-ftc-funeral-rule
The FTC provides information and resources that explain your rights; lists considerations when choosing a funeral provider; and offers questions to ask when making arrangements, comparing products, services and costs.

Selected Independent Funeral Homes
selectedfuneralhomes.org
An international professional association of independent, locally owned funeral homes that adhere to the organization's Code of Good Practice.

National Funeral Directors Association (NFDA)
nfda.org
An international association comprising 19,000 individual members representing more than 10,000 funeral homes in the U.S., Canada, and abroad.

Cremation Association of North America (CANA)
www.cremationassociation.org)
An international association of more than 1,500 funeral homes, funeral directors, crematories, and others. CANA provides statistical data, employee training, and consumer information related to cremation.

Green Burial Council
(greenburialcouncil.org)
The Green Burial Council is an independent, tax-exempt, nonprofit organization working to encourage environmentally sustainable deathcare and the use of burial as a new means of protecting natural areas.

Good Grief Program
bmc.org/pediatrics-goodgrief.htm
For more than 20 years, the Good Grief Program has offered clinical, training, and consultative services to families, educators, health providers, and communities to help adults help children facing life's speed bumps

About the Author

George W. Clarke has more than thirty years' experience in the funeral service industry, beginning as a funeral director/embalmer with a high volume, multi-location funeral home in Massachusetts, and ultimately serving as assistant general manager for the last five years of his thirteen-year tenure. During that time, he personally helped more than 1,000 families arrange appropriate tributes for people they cared about.

In 1991, he accepted a position on an international scale with National Selected Morticians (NSM), known today as Selected Independent Funeral Homes, the world's oldest and largest association of independently owned funeral homes. In that capacity, he was responsible for the association's Management Assistance Program, which provided funeral home management consulting services to the membership.

In 1996, Mr. Clarke was named the association's Executive Director and served in that capacity until August 2007. In that role he designed and implemented membership programs, national public relations campaigns, and legislative initiatives. In regular contact with association members throughout North America and abroad, he was often called upon to contribute his industry experience and expertise to help members resolve management issues and develop best practices. He has also participated in numerous meetings and conferences with representatives of the Bureau of Consumer Protection of the U.S. Federal Trade

Commission regarding its regulation of the funeral industry.

Mr. Clarke has extensive experience in public speaking, has been interviewed by national television and radio outlets regarding funeral industry related issues, and has been quoted extensively in newspaper and magazine articles throughout the United States.

In addition, Mr. Clarke has served as a volunteer for the New England Organ Bank, is a former member of the Board of Directors of the Coalition on Donation (currently known as Donate Life America), and has also served as a volunteer with the Guest Engagement Department of the John G. Shedd Aquarium, Chicago, Illinois.

WWW.CLARKE-RESOURCES.COM

If you would like to learn more about my presentations, discuss arrangements for me to speak to your group, or have any general questions about the subjects of death and funerals, please contact me via the form on my website. I will reply to your inquiry within 24 hours.

Thank you for visiting my website. I look forward to hearing from you.

George W. Clarke
Clarke Resources
7200 1st Ave.
Kenosha, WI 53143
Tel. (866) 835-5018

www.ingramcontent.com/pod-product-compliance
Lightning Source LLC
Chambersburg PA
CBHW032113280326
41933CB00009B/828

* 9 7 8 1 9 3 7 5 9 2 4 0 0 *